RETHINKING
DESIGN
THINKING

AUTHOR/EDITOR/RESEARCHER
GK VanPatter
CoFounder, HUMANTIFIC & NextDesign Leadership Network

VISUAL SENSEMAKING COLLABORATOR
Elizabeth Pastor
CoFounder, HUMANTIFIC & NextDesign Leadership Network

STRATEGIC CONVERSATION COLLABORATOR
Peter Jones, PhD
CoFounder, Redesign Network & RSD Symposium (Relating Systems Thinking and Design)

CONVERSATION CONTRIBUTOR
Anna Barroso

DESIGN: HUMANTIFIC: Evan Dody, Mike Babwahsingh, Amanda Greenough, Tianyi Qi
COPYEDITING: Cathleen McGuire
TYPEFACE: ITC Franklin Gothic BT & Archer

PUBLISHED BY
HUMANTIFIC PUBLISHING
First Edition: January 2020
Copyright © 2020 HUMANTIFIC PUBLISHING, New York

For more information about HUMANTIFIC PUBLISHING, visit www.humantific.com

SERIES: NextD Futures

RETHINKING
DESIGN
THINKING

MAKING SENSE OF THE FUTURE THAT HAS ALREADY ARRIVED

GK VanPatter

Author of INNOVATION METHODS MAPPING:
De-Mystifying 80+ Years of Innovation Process Design

CONTRIBUTORS: Elizabeth Pastor & Peter Jones, PhD

HUMANTIFIC & NextDesign Leadership Network

Advance Praise

"This book shatters assumptions in applying design thinking principles and practices to the rising complexity of challenges and contexts."

 JOAN VINYETS, PhD | REJÓN
Anthropologist, Designer,
Speaker and Entrepreneur

"This book has it spot on—not only about our world being more complex than before, but more importantly, that this demands of us to revisit all we think we are familiar with. Much of what has supported us in the complicated world of the 20th century not only fails to work in the complex 21st century context, it will work against us. While VanPatter is also right in suggesting that we do not know the answers (yet), he is exemplar in leading the way of going on the quest of finding them."

 DR. BETTINA VON STAMM, FRSA
Innovation Leadership Forum
Innovation Philosopher–Story Teller–Catalyst

"As we closed out the 20th century, Humantific was already sounding the alarm over the drive to adopt the pre-framed assumption practice of Design Thinking 1.0 and 2.0 as the panacea to a world facing exponential change and increasingly complex challenges that constitute "non-linear effects from an unknowable multiplicity of factors". Part expose, part history lesson and part provocation, Rethinking Design Thinking takes us through the last two decades and eloquently validates these concerns whilst building the case for Design Thinking 3.0 and 4.0. And even 5.0. The latest edition to Humantific's significant body of work is essential for those faced with leading cohorts of humans (be they organisations, communities, or societies) through the 21st century's Fuzzy Uncertain Complex and Ambiguous world."

 DONNA PATRICIA ANN EIBY
Creative Director,
The Future Work Skills Academy

"Wow, well done. This book has charted a course to a new design future—one that fully embraces co-creation, emergence, and the fuzziness of complexity. I see this as a stepping stone for many others to begin their journey toward co-creating new futures by divesting of the past and embracing new ways. Keep up the wonderful work."

 CHARLES BLACK
CoFounder, Xundis Global

"A thoughtful and beautiful overview of the history and future of design and design thinking. It manages to be both beautiful and profound at the same time! This book belongs on the bookshelf of every student of design and design consultant—especially those tasked with addressing the fuzzy, complex, existential challenges of today.

 PETER COUGHLAN, PhD
Partner, B Economy Partners
formerly partner and CoFounder of IDEO's Transformation by Design practice

"VanPatter, Pastor, and Jones have given us a clear path for the future of design thinking, along with a history of design methodologies. Their roadmap for design thinking is broadly adaptable for complex problems across many situations, and they provide impactful visualizations of the trajectory that they see on the near horizon—along with pointing out what needs to change in order to get there."

 LORRAINE JUSTICE, PhD, FIDSA
Dean Emerita, Professor of Industrial Design, Rochester Institute of Technology
Author, The Future of Design

"ReThinking Design Thinking is a must-read for leaders seeking to harness the full capability of Design Thinking. It should also be the first reading assignment for any design educator. It provides unparalleled clarity for aligning organizational structure and design approaches to the scale of challenge/goal."

 TIM SWEENEY
Founding Partner, Upstream Thinking

"Great book. GK VanPatter and colleagues are some of the sharpest thinkers in the design field. This book is a refreshing and illuminating read clarifying the need for a new approach to design. Excellent, easy to use, illuminating differences between traditional Art and Design approach and multidisciplinary design involving complex situations. I recommend it for design students and lecturers."

DR. TERENCE LOVE
School of Design and Built Environment,
Curtin University, Western Australia
CEO, Design Out Crime and CPTED Centre

"This book is essential reading for design practitioners, professors and students who are: curious to know more about "the elephant in the design thinking living room;" open to reflecting on the value of applying traditional assumption-boxed design methods; and, seriously interested in exploring the gigantic opportunities of moving from design as subservience to design as leadership!"

DR. MARK BRADFORD
Senior Lecturer, Wellington School of
Design, Massey University, New Zealand

"Design thinking has a history and a future. It is not a simple process set and defined. In too many cases, design thinking has become narrowed and blinkered over the past few years. Too much of a simplified process and easy fix. The work of GK VanPatter and Humantific can change this. It connects the past to the future and opens new and grounded approaches to design thinking. This is what we need if we are going to use it as a tool to change our world."

STEVEN FORTH
CoFounder, Ibbaka-TeamFit
Moderator, LinkedIn Design Thinking Group

"What a great book! Refreshing approach and very relevant. Design thinking is much more than meets the eye—multifaceted contexts and the messy world within are explored clearly and visually within this book. The change to externalized mechanisms and the new in-depth considerations are welcome ideas in an era of continual change. Recommended reading for students and educators alike.

TIIU POLDMA, PhD
Professor, Université de Montréal

"This book offers a compelling argument for the "rethinking" of Design Thinking. The best aspect of the book is the way it effortlessly visualizes the shift in challenge, scale, and complexity faced by the design discipline, and makes a compelling argument on why current methods of Design Thinking are failing. It backs up this visual argument with critical conversations that helps deepen our understanding of the topic, and challenges us to rethink our own conception of design. It will be a key resource for helping design students and educators alike to move beyond the product, service, and experience design paradigm."

JOYCE YEE, PhD
Associate Professor,
Northumbria School of Design
CoAuthor, Transformations

"I am obsessed with understanding. My obsession has made the island I live on quite small. There are few people that I allow to dock there, and GK VanPatter is one of those people. He shares my obsession, but on a much deeper level than I am capable of, and with an academic rigor and quality that I don't possess. I guess another way of saying this is that I admire him."

RICHARD SAUL WURMAN

Are you ready to do some rethinking of Design/Design Thinking?

**Open Frame
Design Leader**

This book is dedicated to all those who are open to, and engaged in, **the possibility of reinventing Design/Design Thinking methods** beyond their current state in order to better sync with the rising complexity of challenges in our continuously changing world.

Contents

"Most designers know a lot about the Design 1.0 and Design 2.0 activity spaces. For many the Design 3.0 and Design 4.0 spaces are much more experimental.

What does it mean to take human-centered/life-centered tools into organizational and societal transformation situations?

No one really knows the complete answer to these ongoing questions. These are questions that are being worked on every day in the emerging practice community so that is what makes this terrain interesting to many."

GK VanPatter
Explaining NextDesign Geographies
Reflections on the Arriving Future, 2007

Introduction
HOW THIS JOURNEY BEGAN

Design for complexity is changing Design and Design Thinking.

Is it possible to make sense of a subject that always seems to be in at least ten different places simultaneously along a timeline of evolution? Design and Design Thinking are two such interconnected subjects, so we guessed that taking them on from a sensemaking perspective was not going to be a walk in the park. We guessed right!

Swimming around in these subjects for numerous years we did conclude that such complexity does not prevent us from surfacing some clarity around the challenges facing Design and Design Thinking in the now continuously changing world. This book is an attempt to share the high notes of what we found and what we made sense of.

Concerned about the state of design leadership, Elizabeth Pastor and I began this NextD project journey in 2002 as a community sensemaking initiative outside our Humantific practice. From then until now, we have seen many twists and turns in the road - the popular conversion of Design to Design Thinking among them.

Some of our long-standing readers will know that aspects of this book have been published previously as part of NextD Journal, NextD Library and/or on my personal LinkedIn blog. Here we are combining several summary components that are key to explaining how we make sense of the emerging future of Design, or Design Thinking if you prefer that terminology.

Here in this volume numerous explanation models appear for the first time as well as a new discussion focused on the question of methodology redesign urgency. In addition, we have included 10 Secrets of Design Thinking as well as 25 Ways to Fix Design Thinking for Complex Contexts.

One of the things that we learned in creating this work is that making sense of the present and emerging future of design makes for a complex and somewhat politically charged undertaking. As we presented findings at various conferences, there were moments when we thought we would not publish this book and other moments when we believed it would be helpful to many if it went out the door immediately.

With the shifting sands of the industry there always seemed to be a few pieces missing from the story. Seeing in 2019 that many of the methods - related challenges first pointed out in 2005 still exist, now, in the context of the Design Thinking movement, we decided it was time.

Our intended audience is anyone interested in the many challenges facing Design and Design Thinking not from a philosophical perspective, but rather from a methods and skills one. The acknowledgment of rising challenge complexity - and the embrace of skill-to-scale first pointed out in 2005 remain central to this Rethinking Design and Design Thinking story.

GK VanPatter

10 Secrets of Design Thinking* Today

*Based on the present state of what we call Conventional Design Thinking 2005-2019.

1. Today a mountain of confusion exists in the marketplace around the subject of Design Thinking in part due to the often misleading repackaging of narrowly focused product, service, and experience design methods as broadly focused "Design Thinking."

2. As of 2019, approximately 80-90% of the methods being positioned as "Design Thinking" are in actuality product, service, and experience design methodologies.

3. Often not being made clear in the marketplace, is that product, service and experience methods are assumption-boxed methods. They contain baked-in assumptions regarding both the challenge paths and the solution paths. Such methods are valuable and most suited to contexts where the challenges have already been determined and involve product, service, and/or experience.

4. Often not being made clear in the marketplace is that the starting point for assumption-boxed methods is typically a framed or semi-framed challenge in the form of a "Design Brief."

5. The notion of "Reframing" within assumption-boxed methods typically means reframing within the assumption track...as in reframe functionalities. In such methods, "Reframing" seldom involves rethinking outside the original assumption track.

6. It is widely recognized that the arenas of complex organizational and societal change-making require methods that at the outset, are free of baked-in assumptions regarding what the challenge paths and solution paths might be.

7. A significant gap exists between the notion of highly complex problems - sometimes referred to as "wicked problems"- and the actual, assumption-boxed methods being marketed as Design Thinking today.

8. Adding to the mountain of confusion many of the graduate design academies have for some time been teaching that philosophy is the same as methodology and thus the marketplace contains many folks who have been thus indoctrinated. Today in the marketplace, broad design philosophy is often sold as methodology.

9. Adding to the marketplace confusion, most versions of Design Thinking contain only the explicit aspects of the approach and are missing the deeper tacit knowledge that comes from formal design education and years of practical work experience. Adding even further complexity, the tacit aspects of knowledge that are most present within the industry are primary from the Design 1 and Design 2 Arenas.

10. Conventional Design Thinking methods will require significant redesign in order to better meet the needs of highly complex contexts beyond the assumptions of product, service, or experience design.

"It is important to pause and acknowledge that we are amid the greatest velocity of change in human history, which is compressing time."

Heather E. McGowan
Learning is the New Pension
Forbes, 2019

"The Future is Already Here. It's just not evenly distributed yet."

William Gibson

"The secret of change is to focus all of your energy not on fighting the old, but building the new."

Socrates

What is Design 1.0, 2.0, 3.0, 4.0 Today?

A VISUAL NARRATIVE

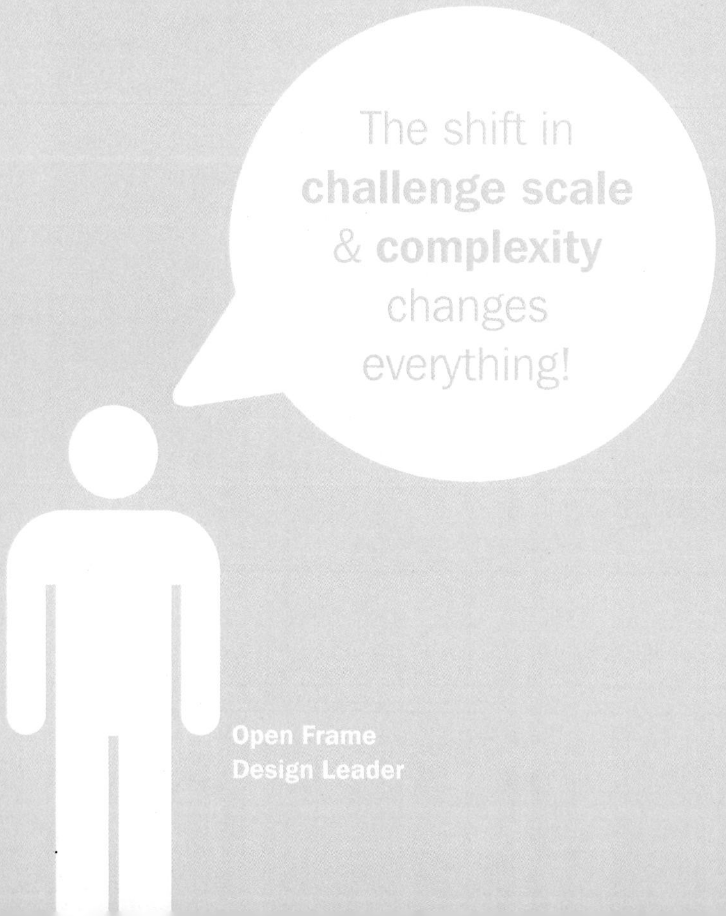

Open Frame
Design Leader

"Today, the **search for and synchronization of tools, methods, and skills to increasing complex problem scale** is a quest underway in many disciplines around the world."

GK VanPatter

Design Thinking is changing.

How big is
the change?

WHAT
designers face
is changing.

COMPLEX
PROBLEMS

Today

Designer

CROSS-DISCIPLINARY TEAM

SINGLE
DISCIPLINE

MULTIPLE
DISCIPLINE

Yesterday

Designer

SIMPLE
PROBLEMS

? What methods, skills,
and tools are needed
to do this work today?

WHEN
design begins
is changing.

Yesterday: Old World Sequential Processing

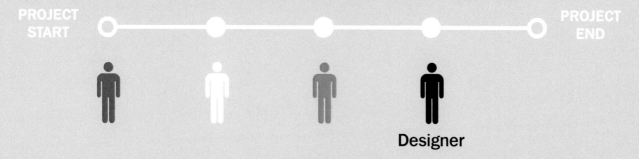

PROJECT START   PROJECT END

Designer

Today: New World Parallel Processing

PROJECT START   PROJECT END

Designer

CROSS-DISCIPLINARY TEAM

? What methods, skills, and tools are needed to do this work today?

HOW
designers work
is changing.

Today

Yesterday

ALONE-WORK

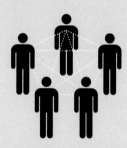

**SINGLE-DISCIPLINE
TEAMWORK**

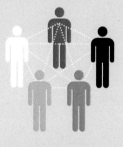

**CROSS-DISCIPLINE
TEAMWORK**

? What methods, skills,
and tools are needed
to do this work today?

The shift in **challenge scale** & **complexity** has significant methodology implications!

Open Frame
Design Leader

Design challenges are shifting!

SHIFT: Small-scale › Large-scale challenges

CHALLENGE
ARENA

1

**SMALL-SCALE
CHALLENGES**

CHALLENGE
ARENA

2

**MEDIUM-SCALE
CHALLENGES**

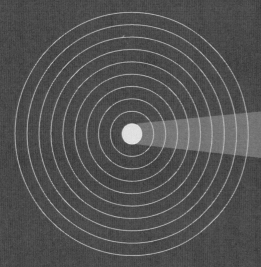 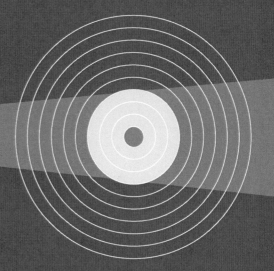

**DESIGN &
DESIGN THINKING**

1.0

**LOGOS
POSTERS
PACKAGING**
CHALLENGES

**DESIGN &
DESIGN THINKING**

2.0

**PRODUCTS
SERVICES
EXPERIENCES**
CHALLENGES

CONVENTIONAL DESIGN THINKING is here

As of 2019, approximately 90% of the methods being framed as DESIGN THINKING are here

Many DESIGN PHILOSOPHIES reflect intention to span this terrain from Design 1.0 to Design 4.0

CHALLENGE
ARENA
3
LARGE-SCALE
CHALLENGES

CHALLENGE
ARENA
4
GIANT-SCALE
CHALLENGES

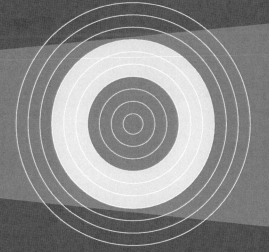

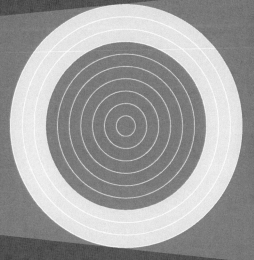

DESIGN &
DESIGN THINKING
3.0
ORGANIZATIONS
SYSTEMS
INDUSTRIES
CHALLENGES

DESIGN &
DESIGN THINKING
4.0
COMMUNITIES
COUNTRIES
PLANET
CHALLENGES

WICKED PROBLEMS are here

CURRENT CONVENTIONAL DESIGN THINKING METHODOLOGY GAP

SHIFT: Simple › Highly complex

CHALLENGE ARENA	CHALLENGE ARENA
1	**2**
SMALL COMPLEXITY	MEDIUM COMPLEXITY

DESIGN & DESIGN THINKING	DESIGN & DESIGN THINKING
1.0	**2.0**
LOGOS POSTERS PACKAGING CHALLENGES	PRODUCTS SERVICES EXPERIENCES CHALLENGES

CONVENTIONAL DESIGN THINKING is here

As of 2019, approximately 90% of the methods being framed as DESIGN THINKING are here

Many DESIGN PHILOSOPHIES reflect intention to span this terrain from Design 1.0 to Design 4.0

CHALLENGE
ARENA
3

LARGE COMPLEXITY

DESIGN &
DESIGN THINKING
3.0

ORGANIZATIONS
SYSTEMS
INDUSTRIES
CHALLENGES

CHALLENGE
ARENA
4

GIANT COMPLEXITY

DESIGN &
DESIGN THINKING
4.0

COMMUNITIES
COUNTRIES
PLANET
CHALLENGES

WICKED PROBLEMS are here

CURRENT CONVENTIONAL DESIGN THINKING METHODOLOGY GAP

SHIFT: Defined challenge › Fuzzy situation

CHALLENGE ARENA	CHALLENGE ARENA
1	**2**
FRAMED CHALLENGES	SEMI-FRAMED CHALLENGES

DESIGN & DESIGN THINKING	DESIGN & DESIGN THINKING
1.0	**2.0**
LOGOS POSTERS PACKAGING CHALLENGES	PRODUCTS SERVICES EXPERIENCES CHALLENGES

CONVENTIONAL DESIGN THINKING is here

As of 2019, approximately 90% of the methods being framed as DESIGN THINKING are here

Many DESIGN PHILOSOPHIES reflect intention to span this terrain from Design 1.0 to Design 4.0

**CHALLENGE
ARENA
3
FUZZY SITUATIONS**

**CHALLENGE
ARENA
4
SUPER FUZZY SITUATIONS**

**DESIGN &
DESIGN THINKING
3.0**

**ORGANIZATIONS
SYSTEMS
INDUSTRIES**
CHALLENGES

**DESIGN &
DESIGN THINKING
4.0**

**COMMUNITIES
COUNTRIES
PLANET**
CHALLENGES

WICKED PROBLEMS are here

CURRENT CONVENTIONAL DESIGN THINKING METHODOLOGY GAP

The shift in **challenge scale & complexity** calls for a serious methods and skills rethink!

Open Frame
Design Leader

How designers work is changing.

SHIFT: Info Hunting › Info SenseMaking

Long before the Big Data era arrived, prescient Information Architect Richard Wurman was pointing out (1980s) a need to get ready for "a tsunami of data crashing on our shores". Standing on the societal sensemaking shoulders of Otto Neurath (1882-1945), Wurman believed optimistically that understanding was a prelude to action in business and societal contexts.

Today the data and information tsunami that Richard identified has grown into an undeniable storm effecting every aspect of business and life. From students to senior executives inside giant global corporations, one of the most important shifts occurring is from the old era activity of hunting for information in the context of info scarcity to needing to continuously make sense in the new era context of continuous information overload.

In practical terms this is a shift of skill, not just a mindset. Approaches to participation and leadership inevitably change with this shift: less hunting coupled with a rise of need for ongoing sensemaking. It's a skill-shift that needs to be - and within the emerging practice community already is being incorporated into Design for Arena 3 and Design for Arena 4.

Yesterday

Today/Tomorrow

EMERGING PRACTICE COMMUNITY is here

Millions of terabytes of data are
generated each day on planet earth*.

Design Team

Design Team

INFO HUNTERS

INFO SENSEMAKERS

Information Hunting in the context
of the old era Information Scarcity

Visual SenseMaking in the context
of new era Information Abundance
and Overload

*It is estimated that by 2025 there will be
463 million terabytes of data generated each day
on planet earth. Source: Internet

SHIFT: Activity Emphasis

CHALLENGE
ARENA
1

CHALLENGE
ARENA
2

SENSEmaking **STRANGE**making

Making differentiated
objects

SENSEmaking **STRANGE**making

Making differentiated
objects

Toolbox 1

Toolbox 2

CONVENTIONAL DESIGN THINKING is here

As of 2019, approximately 90% of the methods being framed as DESIGN THINKING are here

Many DESIGN PHILOSOPHIES reflect intention to span this terrain from Design 1.0 to Design 4.0

CHALLENGE
ARENA
3

CHALLENGE
ARENA
4

SENSEmaking **CHANGE**making

Making Change in
organizations

SENSEMaking **CHANGE**making

Making change in
societies

Toolbox 3

Toolbox 4

WICKED PROBLEMS are here

CURRENT CONVENTIONAL DESIGN THINKING METHODOLOGY GAP

SHIFT: Intuition/Evidence/Insights

Interconnected to the rise of information abundance is the shift away from 100% intuitive approaches to Design/Design Thinking and the integration of various forms of evidence/insights into designerly methods for complex contexts.

Evidence/Insights is recognized as a much bigger category than data alone and incorporates various forms of social-science generated insights. Highly complex problems cannot be adequately tackled with intuitive force alone. In the context of Design for Arena 3 and Arena 4, intuition does not disappear, but it is now reproportioned with a high degree of evidence and insight.

In our Humantific practice we have long been interested in the method related impact of information abundance. In the next generation emerging practice community various approaches to evidence/insight integration into methodology can already be found. Part of the challenge is to update/reinvent design research in order to make its application and output applicable to a broader range of complex situations beyond product, service, and experience assumptions.

Yesterday

Today/Tomorrow

EMERGING PRACTICE COMMUNITY is here

EVIDENCE

INTUITION

INTUITION

EVIDENCE

Design Team Journey

Design Team Journey

OLD ERA

DESIGN AS
INTUITION
INSPIRED JOURNEY

NEW ERA

DESIGN AS
EVIDENCE/INSIGHT
INFORMED JOURNEY

SHIFT: Starting Points

UPSTREAM METHODS

Open-Aperture
Assumption-Free

UNDEFINED CHALLENGE
(FUZZY SITUATION)

SEMI-DEFINED CHALLENGE
(BRIEF)

DEFINED CHALLENGE
(BRIEF)

DOWNSTREAM METHODS

Assumption-Boxed

Most of the current design industry, including graduate design education, is here

DESIGN & DESIGN THINKING 1.0	DESIGN & DESIGN THINKING 2.0	DESIGN & DESIGN THINKING 3.0	DESIGN & DESIGN THINKING 4.0

FUZZY SITUATION	UNDEFINED CHALLENGE	UNDEFINED CHALLENGE	**UNDEFINED** CHALLENGE	**UNDEFINED** CHALLENGE
BRIEF	SEMI-DEFINED CHALLENGE	**SEMI-DEFINED** CHALLENGE	SEMI-DEFINED CHALLENGE	SEMI-DEFINED CHALLENGE
BRIEF	**DEFINED** CHALLENGE	DEFINED CHALLENGE	DEFINED CHALLENGE	DEFINED CHALLENGE

STARTING POINT: Jumps off from **BRIEF** (Framed Challenge)	STARTING POINT: Jumps off from **BRIEF** (Semi-Framed Challenge)	STARTING POINT: Jumps off from **FUZZY SITUATION**	STARTING POINT: Jumps off from **FUZZY SITUATION**

These methods are ASSUMPTION-BOXED

They contain challenge and outcome assumptions upfront

By design these methods are ASSUMPTION-FREE

They don't contain challenge or outcome assumptions upfront

See: *Explaining Design Geographies*, page 50-59

SHIFT: Methods Language

DESIGN &
DESIGN THINKING
1.0

DESIGN &
DESIGN THINKING
2.0

METHOD LANGUAGE A: Process and content knowledge are **combined** in one role

CONTENT   PROCESS

MIXED MODE
Content & Process
Undifferentiated Mixed

CONTENT   PROCESS

MIXED MODE
Content & Process
Undifferentiated Mixed

CONVENTIONAL DESIGN THINKING is here

DESIGN & DESIGN THINKING **3.0**	DESIGN & DESIGN THINKING **4.0**

MIXED MODE
Content & Process
Undifferentiated Mixed

MIXED MODE
Content & Process
Undifferentiated Mixed

METHOD LANGUAGE B: Content role can be **different** from process role

SPLIT MODE
Content & Process
Differentiated Split

SPLIT MODE
Content & Process
Differentiated Split

Approaches in these Arenas contain two Method Language types

SHIFT: Philosophy/Methodology

Yesterday/Today

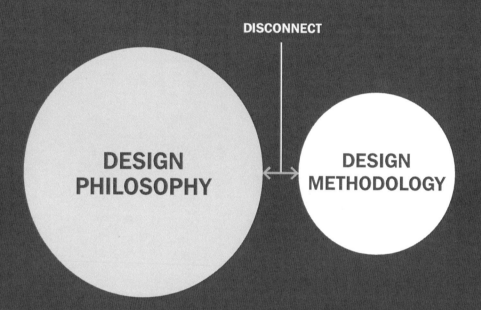

DISCONNECT

DESIGN PHILOSOPHY

DESIGN METHODOLOGY

DESIGN PHILOSOPHY SAYS:

Design can address any kind of problem, even massive wicked problems

DESIGN METHODOLOGY SAYS:

Design Methods presume product, service, experience challenges and outcomes

These methods unable to deliver on this promise

Today/Tomorrow

EMERGING PRACTICE COMMUNITY is here

ALIGNED

DESIGN PHILOSOPHY

REDESIGNED DESIGN METHODOLOGY FOR COMPLEX CONTEXTS

DESIGN PHILOSOPHY SAYS:

Design can address any kind of problem, even massive wicked problems

DESIGN METHODOLOGY SAYS:

Design Methods & skills differ across the Challenge Arenas

These methods being redesigned to deliver on this promise

SHIFT: Stakeholders/Team

**DESIGN &
DESIGN THINKING**

1.0

Hidden Magical Methodology
("Wave the wand")

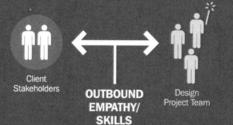

Designers as Main Agents

Client
Stakeholders

**OUTBOUND
EMPATHY/
SKILLS**

Design
Project Team

TOOLBOX 1

Outcomes:	100% emergent
Facts:	100% emergent
Methods:	90% emergent

ATTRIBUTES
- No Externalized Process
- 99% Intuitive
- Might or Might Not Contain
  Evidence-Informed Orientation

**FEW
STAKEHOLDERS**

These downstream methods are not visualized.
They are focused on outbound considerations.

DESIGN &
DESIGN THINKING
2.0

Externalized Methodology

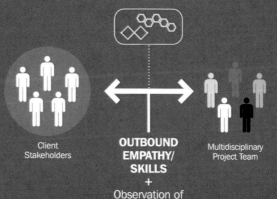

Designers as Main Agents

Client
Stakeholders

**OUTBOUND
EMPATHY/
SKILLS
+**
Observation of
Human Behavior

Multidisciplinary
Project Team

TOOLBOX 2

Outcomes:	100% emergent
Facts:	100% emergent
Methods:	10% emergent

ATTRIBUTES
- Assumes Product / Service / Experience Challenges
- Assumes Product / Service / Experience Outcomes
- Product / Service / Experience Design Orientation
- Product / Service / Experience Scale
- Product / Service / Experience Design Process
- Might or Might Not Contain Evidence-Informed Orientation

These downstream methods are often visualized
and focused on outbound user insights.

SHIFT: Stakeholders/Team

**DESIGN &
DESIGN THINKING**

Externalized Methodology
Outbound & Inbound Tools
Interconnected

- Strategy
- Methods
- Thinking Styles

Designers Lead Co-Creation

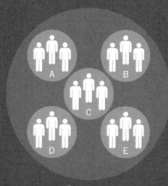

Organization

**MANY
STAKEHOLDERS**

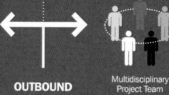

Multidisciplinary
Project Team

**INBOUND
EMPATHY/
SKILLS**
+
Improving Team
Dynamics
&
Team Creation
&
Inclusive Culture
Building

**OUTBOUND
EMPATHY/
SKILLS**
+
Observation of
Human Behavior
&
Participatory
Co-Creation

TOOLBOX 3

Outcomes:	100% emergent
Facts:	100% emergent
Methods:	25% emergent

ATTRIBUTES
- Open Assumption Free Framing
- Adaptable Orientation
- Adaptable Scale
- Adaptable Process
- Evidence-Informed Orientation

These methods are visualized and contain outbound
and inbound skills connected to culture building.

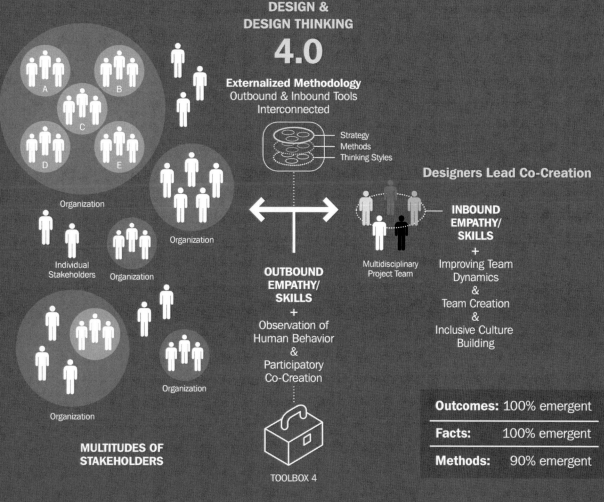

DESIGN & DESIGN THINKING

4.0

Externalized Methodology
Outbound & Inbound Tools
Interconnected

- Strategy
- Methods
- Thinking Styles

Designers Lead Co-Creation

INBOUND EMPATHY/ SKILLS
+
Improving Team Dynamics
&
Team Creation
&
Inclusive Culture Building

Multidisciplinary Project Team

Organization

Organization

Individual Stakeholders

Organization

OUTBOUND EMPATHY/ SKILLS
+
Observation of Human Behavior
&
Participatory Co-Creation

Organization

Organization

Organization

MULTITUDES OF STAKEHOLDERS

Outcomes:	100% emergent
Facts:	100% emergent
Methods:	90% emergent

TOOLBOX 4

ATTRIBUTES
- Open Assumption Free Framing
- Adaptable Orientation
- Adaptable Scale
- Adaptable Process
- Evidence-Informed Orientation

MANY STAKEHOLDERS

These methods are visualized and contain outbound
and inbound skills connected to culture building.

"Human-centered design is great for mops and phones, but [in its current conventional state] it won't solve society's biggest problems."

Jesse Weaver
Design Won't Save The World
2019

"Today this job isn't about helping Nike sell shoes. Its about making sure everyone has shoes."

Mike Monteiro
Ruined by Design
2019

"An obsession with efficiency, researchers have discovered, can come at the expense of invention."

Oliver Staley
What Ever Happened to Six Sigma?
2019

Overview Conversations/ Essays

THE DESIGN 1.0, 2.0, 3.0, 4.0 JOURNEY

Explaining NextDesign Geographies

REFLECTIONS ON THE ARRIVING FUTURE

IN CONVERSATION

GK VanPatter
CoFounder, Humantific, New York
CoFounder, NextDesign Leadership Network

Peter Jones, PhD
Redesign Network
Associate Professor, Strategic Foresight and Innovation, OCAD University
CoFounder, Systemic Design Association, RSD Symposium

Conversation originally published in 2007

Peter Jones: GK, as you know the interactions community is comprised of user experience and interaction designers, human-centered researchers, academic researchers, and other design professionals. However, I have never seen anything like your theory of change in design practice described in these pages. Let us assume most readers may not have encountered Design 3.0 or Design 4.0. May I ask you to start with an overview of your perspective of the historical changes happening around the design professions?

GK VanPatter: We have many friends in the interactions community and I am delighted to do this. In reference to an overview of historical changes in design practice: Let me suggest an overview of an overview for this compressed format. Let me start by saying that what we do at NextD is not create theories, but rather provide synthesis of what we see occurring all around us. The dots are there. We just connect them.

When Elizabeth Pastor and I launched NextD as an experiment in 2002, we did not know exactly what it was we were looking at in the marketplace and in academia, but we had general concerns about the state of design leadership, that it was falling behind and was badly out of sync with the real world that we were familiar with at that time. We knew from our practice that "design" was, for numerous reasons, changing rapidly and significantly, but we did not see much evidence of this in graduate design education. Quite frankly, much of American design education did not seem to understand the massive continuous change occurring outside of design. We were not the owners of this problem, but we thought it might be useful to lend a hand since we both come from design backgrounds.

> For a number of reasons we felt that pitching in to help would be useful to a community that is near and dear to us and one that we will always be part of.

Since the term "design" is so loaded, we initially considered proceeding with this rethinking exercise under a different terminology banner. For ten years, Humantific has gone to market as an innovation enabling company, not a design company. For us going back, or sideways so to speak, to rethink design was somewhat of a counter intuitive exercise. For a number of reasons we felt that pitching in to help would be useful to a community that is near and dear to us and one that we will always be part of.

In 2002, it appeared that design education leaders and the leaders of the professional design associations were missing in action regarding the rethinking of design, so we jumped in. It is important to understand that NextD was created as a sensemaking and changemaking experiment, not a design promotion initiative. Upon launch we described the traditional model of design leadership as a burning platform. Not everyone appreciated that view.

From the outset we focused on how we might utilize sensemaking to convey in specific terms what was changing and why change was needed. To do this we undertook sensemaking conversations with many thoughtful people from inside and outside of design. With a ReRethinking Design orientation, NextD Journal began creating authentic views into the conditions of design and also illuminated new paths for designers.

Along the way in that journey we learned a tremendous amount about the design community, interconnected communities, and the various forces in play in the marketplace - what was changing, what was not. Being a seasoned professional yourself I think you must know that not all of what was encountered was pleasant. To be frank, the competitive marketplace that now includes design education, design practice, and professional design associations can be brutal. In NextD Journal conversations we saw some thought leaders questioning whether there was a design community at all. Encountering this community context reminded us that this kind of changemaking work is not for the faint of heart.

After several years of sharing in-depth thought leadership conversations, NextD created several sensemaking frameworks, including Design 1.0, 2.0, and 3.0 which was launched at the national AIGA conference in 2005. We recognized that it is impossible to have a meaningful conversation about the changing nature of design today without some kind of sensemaking framework. With many well-meaning government leaders around the world trying to figure out how to make use of their design communities in the face of globalization, we wanted to provide a few simple dialogue tools.

The NextDesign Geographies Framework is in essence a complexity scale. It is a post-discipline view that is process, not content focused. As a field of knowledge, design is an amorphous time warp that exists across several time zones or paradigms simultaneously. Some are old rather static paradigms while others are transforming and/or just emerging. Unlike in traditional science, the various paradigms of design do not necessarily replace each other as they emerge. As practice and study zones, the paradigms within design exist in parallel. The various operational states of design exist simultaneously. There are often competing and conflicting interests between the zones which tends to generate a lot of heat in the marketplace.

We figured out early on that the best way to explain the degree of change occurring inside and outside of design was to focus on how the scale of challenges facing us in the real world were changing.

We recognized that it is impossible to have a meaningful conversation about the changing nature of design today without some kind of sensemaking framework.

In our conference and workshop talks we attempt to place the change in everyday work context: We point out that if one was trained to tackle poster-sized framed challenges, it is likely that new skills and tools will be required to tackle highly complex fuzzy challenges like organizational transformation or world peace. We point out that globalization ie: the off-shoring, shrinking, and commoditization of once thriving North American design markets is driving a strategic space race. The reality is that design educated designers now have to compete for design and/or innovation leadership roles. To say this another way, the question of who frames the challenges in the strategic space upstream from briefs has become a hugely competitive aspect of the market. It is a relatively simple message.

The truth is when we started presenting the Design 1.0, Design 2.0, Design 3.0 framework at conferences in 2005, it was controversial as the two most high profile graduate schools in this country were busy selling product design as the future of design. In addition, the then high-flying new business press was closely aligned with the product-centric Design 2.0 view, busily encouraging designers to be gleeful about chasing the next iPod. In presenting the existence of an emerging Design 3.0 organizational transformation design community in 2005, we were already pointing out that many of the challenges facing organizations, facing our communities cannot be solved by creating more products, services, or related experiences however human-centered they might be. Product creation is often a solution to a problem that 21st century humans do not have.

> When it comes to design, the wheels of change are often moving faster outside the United States. NextD has always been focused in the global design community.

Although our perspective has made NextD controversial in some local design community circles, it has also generated high interest among global readers not smitten with the American product-centric perspective. When it comes to design, the wheels of change are often moving faster outside the United States. NextD has always been focused in the global design community. Today the synchronization of tools and skills to problem scale is a quest underway in most disciplines around the world. No graduate school and few practices can escape that reckoning.

Peter Jones: You and I have spoken at some length about the different orientations to the collaborative design skill we call sensemaking, a critical emerging skill and fairly recent perspective in the design field, which has been dominated by the model of individual designer model of branding and differencing. How could experience designers start to incorporate sensemaking into the context of large product/service design projects?

GK VanPatter: These are difficult questions to properly address in this compressed format. Of all the issues in the mix around the changing nature of design today, the rise and transformation of sensemaking is, from our perspective, among the most important elements of the story.

At Humantific, we distinguish between making the strange familiar and making the familiar strange. As a scholar you might recognize this two-part terminology as it can be found in William JJ Gordon's original 1950s-60s era Synectics work. Anyone who has studied the history of the applied creativity movement will know that Gordon was among the 20th century pioneers of this knowledge domain. He was interested in developing new creative methods and the development of deliberate creative capacity in humans. In the context of your question it is important to recognize that Gordon was working on and modeling such issues long before the later generation sensemaking pioneers arrived in the 1970s, 80s, and 90s. Early on we saw in Gordon's work a methodological orientation seed that remains central to our approach to sensemaking today. At Humantific, we call making the strange familiar, sensemaking and making the familiar strange, strangemaking. Like Gordon, we recognize both dimensions as an interconnected continuous cycle linked to innovation. We have built our somewhat oddball, hybrid Humantific practice on the exploration and examination of the interconnections between sensemaking and strangemaking, which is in organizational and societal contexts also called changemaking. For more than ten years, Elizabeth and I have been working at the intersection between the two, so at this point we understand well how they are connected.

In 1998, I wrote my first paper on differences and similarities between organizational sensemaking, the understanding business, and innovation enabling while working for Richard Saul Wurman. We were working on a large innovation ecology project in intervention mode, so we had to figure out how to explain what we were proposing and doing to organizational leaders who had been reading Karl Weick.

Today information processing is only one dimension of the kinds of sensemaking that are already operationalized in next generation design-oriented practices.

In that era there was significant emphasis on the human capacity to process what Wurman described as "a tsunami of data crashing on our shores." At that time very smart people from information science, organizational psychology, cognitive science, knowledge management, and many other fields were working on various aspects of information processing in humans and in organizations without always having views into each other's work. Part of my job at that time was to synthesize and explain how the various streams might be interconnected.

Coming from very different backgrounds, Dervin, Weick, and Wurman were focused in one way or another in the direction of human information processing. Most of those streams were underway in the context of academic study and research. In contrast, Wurman and the understanding business folks were among the first to make sensemaking into a form of practice. Still today these areas of study and work remain largely blind to each other, unless you are deliberately looking across these streams. From our perspective they inform each other.

Since those early years, much has changed in the world and certainly in practice.

We have built steadily on those early foundations. To compress a lot of learning and complexity into a few short sentences: It took us many years to figure out that what organizations and humans in general are trying to do in the 21st century is not just process mountains of data, but make sense of complex fuzzy situations of all kinds, often before any data exists. Today information processing is only one dimension of the kinds of sensemaking that are already operationalized in next generation design oriented practices.

It also took us a long time to figure out (and be able to explain) the correlation between the rise of complexity facing planet earth and the parallel interest in more robust forms of sensemaking. In retrospect it is quite obvious. The good news is that the proportion of sensemaking to changemaking shifts as challenges grow in complexity. In the context of highly complex fuzzy messes, there is most often a need to do significant sensemaking before changemaking begins. If we are working on a tiny problem this is not likely the case. In its various forms, sensemaking now plays a key role on the fuzzy front-end of most significant innovation and change initiatives, in organizations, and in society. This shift has significant implications for future design education.

In our Complexity Navigation Program, business executives learn a five-dimensional model of sensemaking that includes how to make sense of the opportunity/problem space, the humans in the space, the information in the space, the problem owners and the project team. As you point out in your question, the activity of co-creation is at the center of a lot of sensemaking today. Often we are creating cognitive scaffolds that accelerate and enable collective sensemaking. To do this requires a much different kind of approach and a different toolbox than those in use in traditional design oriented practices.

I don't think it is any secret that our design education institutions have for decades been teaching what amounts to a huge emphasis on strangemaking. The branding business is all about strangemaking as one toothbrush, bottle of water, website is made to be different from another as a form of value. Strangemaking is about differencing. For a long time there has been a public perception that differencing is the value add that design brings to the party. Today the design industries contain zillions of people focused on differencing services. It is a huge business that sustains many companies. We always felt a little odd at design conferences as we were designers in the sense-making business. Much to our surprise, as complexity continues to rise, the outside has become the inside. Today sensemaking, inclusive of design research, strategic co-creation, and visual sensemaking is at the center of the revolution within design thinking, innovation, transformation - whatever you choose to call it. It is the change inside the change.

With invitations to join various groups overflowing, soon there will be social innovation initiative fatigue no doubt.

Regarding the other part of your question about what UX practitioners can do: In these economic times, with a lot of web related work already off-shore, for some the question is not how to do the same thing better, but instead how to help their companies better address difficult challenges and become more adaptable to change. We have worked with several experience design focused groups to help them rethink their mission and their value in the context of what their organizations now face. They are essentially working on how might they become more strategically useful to their companies. If you put your adaptability hat on, the good news is that the sensing and sensemaking aspects of UX can be updated and re-purposed. If you look closely at the present leading firms in the shrinking and commoditizing UX space, this is essentially what they are trying to do. Many are working hard on getting themselves into the strategic space. Some seem to have no clue what that really means in terms of skills and tools, but there is no question that this is where they are headed. For those who choose to do the same thing better or differently, new forms of sensemaking add significant value to the front end of any innovation effort, including those focused on user experience design.

Peter Jones: As I know your work, I'm aware that you have been extending the model to include Design 4.0, which may be a nascent weak signal on the horizon for most practitioners. How might we become aware of the need for Design 4.0 thinking in our design and organizational contexts? Simply put, what does this mean to most of us?

GK VanPatter: Last week at the EXPOSED conference held in the Arizona State University School of Design I presented Design 1.0, 2.0, 3.0, 4.0/Understanding Futures that have Already Arrived. It was the first time we have presented Design 4.0/Social Transformation Design.

I do like your descriptive term "nascent weak signal on the horizon." I think that is a generally true depiction. However we are seeing a lot more action in the Design 4.0 activity space than what might have been imagined only a year ago. Anyone on Facebook will know that there are already a dozen social innovation-related initiatives being launched every month on that platform. With invitations to join various groups overflowing, soon there will be social innovation initiative fatigue no doubt.

What we are likely seeing is the first post-911, post-Inconvenient Truth, post-World Changing cycle of social innovation initiatives move through the social network system complete with a lot of energy, enthusiasm, and probably a certain amount of naiveté regarding many of these highly complex social challenges facing occupants of planet earth. The social networking platforms are making it easy to launch and get started. Apart from the excessive exuberance around social innovation, what is actually going on seems a little more messy and complicated as life tends to be. At NextD, we try to look at what the activity occurring under the banner of social innovation actually is from a methods perspective. Although no perfect lens exists the NextD complexity scale helps us in this regard.

So far much of what is going on seems to be what we call Cross-Overs.

In the Design 4.0 activity space, we see multitudes of branded and unbranded approaches that can be grouped into five basic categories:

The Algorithm Group
Network-based up or down voting and data patterns analysis

The Science of Dialogue Design Group
Technology-enabled, transformation-focused dialogue

The Transformation by Design Group
Hybrid toolbox applied to social change

The Problem Solving Group
Creative problem solving applied to social change

The Cross-Over Group
Design 1.0 and Design 2.0 methods applied to social change

The groups vary in terms of size and focus. From what we see, the Algorithm Group is working on various network platforms focused primarily in the direction of "decision-making." How might they harness the power of the democratic collective is what this group seems to be interested in presently. The present web works best for up or down judging - a giant judges table. Presently in Algorithm Group literature, there is much less focus on where the ideas are going to come from. Wouldn't it be interesting to see the change patterns around how the public feels about Obama today, next year, and four years from now? These are issues of interest to this group or group of groups as there are many different streams involved. The tricky part is that while global society has never had such technologies, we already know that there is a lot more to transformation than judging. How do we get to social transformation from collective judging? The tremendous amount of unstudied terrain here will certainly keep graduate students and practitioners busy for years to come.

The Science of Dialogue Design Group, Transformation by Design Group, and The Problem Solving Group are more action, intervention, or design-enabling-focused and seek in several different ways to engage multiple constituents upstream from briefs without any preconceived notions of what the problems and solutions might be. They seek to enable collective and individual ideation, judging, decision-making, and change related action. This is quite different from just focusing on judgment. Without getting into describing the various toolboxes, some are digital, some are analogue, and some are combined. The emphasis among these groups tends to be on process rather than content. There is a lot of energy around this group today as it is being transformed with new hybrid tools and practices.

As far as we know, no one has yet gathered any scientific numbers on these activities, but we are guessing that the Cross-Over Group is probably the largest, growing rapidly as many young generation designers actively seek meaningful work and engage with their existing skills and toolsets.

There seems to be a lot of young generation designers not wanting to engage in chasing the next iPod in Chicago or Hong Kong. Instead, many want to somehow engage with their mindset and tool set in more socially meaningful work in Africa and other countries in need. Inevitably embedded in Cross-Over social innovation initiatives are the methods from Design 1.0 and/or Design 2.0 where high degrees of co-creation, framing, and sensemaking have historically not been front and center. In many Cross-Overs, designers are working in a social context, but what they are really doing is still Design 1.0 or Design 2.0 work.

The tremendous amount of unstudied terrain here will certainly keep graduate students and practitioners busy for years to come.

In Cross-Overs, one can see a lot of assumptions being made that exporting Design 1.0 and Design 2.0 is what we need to do to help in Africa, etc. With the best of intentions there is often the ingrained predeposition that products and services are the solutions needed. Although this might often be the case, in some situations and in some countries it might not be. We already know from complex multiple constituents, Design 3.0 work that preframing assumptions upfront is a problematic recipe.

There are many ways to undertake Cross-Overs. Last year, Humantific's Understanding Lab was involved in the Measure of America, the first human development report focused on a developed country. This was essentially a social sensemaking initiative at the scale of a country, the USA. We were engaged to make the research understandable and engaging as part of a broader social changemaking initiative that is still underway. Here we built what amounted to sensemaking acceleration tools that government leaders and others now use to clearly spell out the need for social change in this country. In that kind of project we focus on fact-finding illumination and problem reframing rather than on driving specific solutions. We see numerous constructive ways to undertake Cross-Overs.

Generally in Design 3.0 and Design 4.0 there is more need for open challenge framing, more need for deep local human-centered sensemaking.

The design community seems to be in the midst of a Cross-Over wave. In all the enthusiasm few seem to be asking if this approach is really working, but we have no doubt that such questions will arise as the various initiatives unfold. It is still very early in that cycle. The lessons and realizations will no doubt in time be emergent!

Most designers know a lot more about the Design 1.0 and Design 2.0 activity spaces, so for many, the Design 3.0 and Design 4.0 spaces are much more experimental.

It does seem unlikely that simply exporting Design 1.0 and Design 2.0 to developing countries will in itself solve world hunger, world peace, and the multitude of other wicked problems facing our collective selves.

Presently, there are a lot less design-oriented folks operating in the fuzzy frontend of social transformation design where challenges are co-created and framed far upstream from briefs. I know that you have been involved in the "Dialogue Design" arena for some years so you probably see this yourself. Design 3.0 and Design 4.0 work tends to involve multiple constituents and quite different challenge types. Upstream from where Design 1.0 and Design 2.0 jump off from, these challenges are more fuzzy, more complex, and involve many constituents so a different toolbox is needed.

Most designers know a lot more about the Design 1.0 and Design 2.0 activity spaces, so for many, the Design 3.0 and Design 4.0 spaces are much more experimental. What does it mean to take human-centered tools into organizational and social transformation situations? No one really knows the complete answer to these ongoing questions. These, are questions that are being worked on everyday in practice, so that is what makes this terrain interesting to many.

To a significant degree Design 3.0 and Design 4.0 still represent relatively undiscovered countries for many with design backgrounds, but that too is rapidly changing as globalization takes hold and drives change in the design community.

Ten years from now, I think many more will be engaged in the Design 3.0 and Design 4.0 activity spaces with more knowledge and better tools. Certainly many smart people are hard at work on this around the world.

Peter Jones: Considering the models you've disclosed, can you further illuminate how designers inspired by the possibilities of transformation design and sustainable design might adopt these distinctions and put them to work in real practice situations?

GK VanPatter: The NextD message is quite simple: The changes underway outside of design are due to the very real forces of globalization that exist in the marketplace. It is not rocket science to point out that as the market changes many design oriented firms are proactively adapting to change.

Some design markets are shrinking while others are emerging. What is going on around Design 3.0 and Design 4.0 is not someone's cool idea. It is change in response to change. Those in the various design communities can draw their own conclusions regarding how or if they see that change and how or if they want to change. Change is occurring whether everyone likes it or not.

REFERENCES

Weick, Karl E. *Sensemaking in Organizations.* Sage Publications, 1995.
Dervin, Brenda. *From the Minds Eye of the User: The Sense-Making Qualitative, Quantitative Methodology. J. D. Glazier & R.R. Powell (Eds),* Qualitative Research in Information Management, Englewood, CO: Libraries Unlimited, 1992.
Wurman, Richard Saul. *Information Anxiety.* Bantam Doubleday, 1989.
Weick, Karl E. *Enacted Sensemaking in Crisis Situations.* Journal of Management Studies, 1988.
Gordon, William JJ. *Synectics, The Development of Creative Capacity.* Collier Books, 1961.

NOTE
This interview was originally published in 2005 as a special edition of NextD Journal after the then editors of Interaction Magazine with competing interests of their own turned it down unless we removed all of the references to NextD and Humantific. We declined and published the interview ourselves.

Origins of NextDesign Geographies

WHY THE FRAMEWORK WAS CREATED

IN CONVERSATION

GK VanPatter
CoFounder, Humantific, New York
CoFounder, NextDesign Leadership Network

Ana Barroso
Founder, The Thinking School

Conversation originally published in 2007

Ana Barroso: Thanks for agreeing to do this Brazil-New York conversation.

For numerous years I have been watching Humantific do sensemaking work focused on the rather fuzzy subject of design/design thinking. How are you able to do that? How did you create the sensemaking frameworks that you use to decipher and explain the various forms of design/design thinking that you refer to as Design 1.0, 2.0, 3.0, 4.0?

GK VanPatter: Hi Ana. Happy to do this in a sharable way. Delighted to see you revving up your interest in sensemaking. Upon your suggestion, I did take a look at the "Why everyone is a designer" article. No big surprises there.

Yes, I would be happy to start by briefly explaining where the sensemaking framework of NextD Geographies came from, how and why it was created. Hopefully this will be of interest to sensemaking readers and it might also come in handy when we get to Mr. Treder's article. :-)

The practice-based view that we have on the subject of design/design thinking today has been informed by more than a decade of work with organizational leaders, in particular the sensemaking research that we undertook via the NextDesign Leadership project intermittently. That is essentially a community sensemaking project that grew out of a concern regarding the state of graduate design education and design leadership.

> After a couple of years of NextD Journal conversations, we were ready to make sense of what we were seeing and hearing.

As background to the design thinking models and frameworks that you see us sharing via NextD, we conducted 30+ community-based sensemaking conversations with numerous experts over the course of several years. That research informed much of what is depicted in the various NextDesign Leadership materials that remain accessible in the NextD Futures Library located on Issuu.

After a couple of years of NextD Journal conversations, we were ready to make sense of what we were seeing and hearing. As sensemakers we knew that some kind of ordering system framework was going to be needed to tell the story. For readers who might not know, ordering systems are integral to the sensemaking business. A central pillar in our Humantific practice is that sensemaking and changemaking are interconnected, that the effective making sense of a subject will serve to inform changemaking.

As we do in all sensemaking projects, we first ask if any such ordering systems exist among the expertise of the subject. If we are doing a futures-related project, we would ask how professional futurists organize the future. We might or might not use their ordering logic, but we would want to look at various existing frameworks. We also look in other subjects for possible related sensemaking frameworks. Some sensemaking-oriented readers might know that years ago Richard Wurman created an ordering system framework for ordering systems. Known as LATCH it consists of Location, Alphabet, Time, Category, Hierarchy. These are universal basics that we keep in mind as we consider ordering logic options.

The Latch Model, Source: *Richard Saul Wurman*

If nothing that we see in existing ordering frameworks suit the findings that are embedded in the research, then typically we know that it will be necessary to somehow create a new ordering framework, adapt an existing one, or combine several. This applies to all the sensemaking projects that we do at Humantific, not just this NextDesign Leadership project - and we do hundreds of projects every year.

Frameworks are considered the scaffolds that help to structure research findings in order to clearly tell related stories. The emphasis is typically not on the framework, but rather on the story within, what the various findings convey.

Central to what the design community research revealed to us was that there were multiple disconnects between the challenges that exist in organizations and societies, what the graduate design schools were teaching at the level of methods, and what emerging practices were already working on, what skills were already needed. At that time and still today there was a heavy emphasis on product/service design in graduate design education. People were using fancy words like "wicked problems," but what was really being taught from a methods perspective was most often product/service creation.

The NextD research revealed significant marketplace shifts, a strategic design practice revolution and a highly complex design education mess that in large measure still exists today. Our task in that moment was to figure out a way to visualize what we learned from a methods perspective. We needed an organizing framework that made sense in this context.

In terms of ordering systems that might be applicable we knew that complexity ladders of numerous types existed in several subjects. The complexity scale idea has deep historical roots and was certainly not unique to our project or to design ecology..:-) If you Google complexity scales or complexity ladders thousands of versions come up spanning not decades but centuries.

Complexity Scale, 16th century depiction, Great Chain of Being, Source: *Internet*

Aristotle (384-322 BC) is credited with creating numerous influential ordering systems including "Great Chain of Being"/ "Ladder of Life" ("Scala Naturae"), an early hierarchy-based classification of organisms, ranking humans, animals, and plants according to complexity of their structure and function.

Compressing hundreds of years of history, suffice it to say that since 330 BC, zillions of other sensemaking thinkers have adopted and adapted the complexity scale idea to various subject contexts.

While we didn't have to agree or disagree with them all, we were certainly aware that many complexity scale adaptations exist. Acknowledging that history, we knew that the orientation of ranking organism complexity was not the focus of our design community research findings. :-) We were interested in the implications of problem or challenge complexity scale.

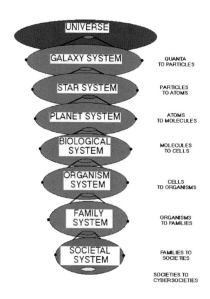

Complexity Scale, Source: *Internet*

Like complexity ladder frameworks many problem scale ladders can also be found by a simple Google search. Organizing systems denoting numbered dimensions of 1, 2, 3, 4, 5, etc. are quite common in sensemaking land across the spectrum of many subjects including problem solving.

Problem-size/scale frameworks often map to logic developed and refined in the Applied Creativity (Creative Problem Solving/CPS) community known as "Ladder of Abstraction," today also referred to as challenge mapping, strategic challenge framing, etc.

HOW BIG IS THE PROBLEM?

Emergency!	-Earthquake -Blood or broken bone -Someone's hurting me	5
Huge	-Parents are divorcing -Grandparent is very sick -Pet died	4
Big	-A kid bit me -Can't do my work -Feel really sick	3
Medium	-Argued with friend -Forgot homework -A kid called me a name	2
Small	-Had to clip down -Someone cut me in line -5 minutes on the bench	1
Glitch	-Don't have a pencil -Indoor recess -Teacher didn't call on me	0

Problem Scale, Source: *Internet*

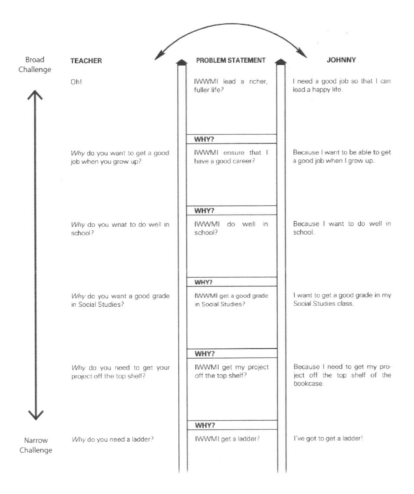

CPS Ladder of Abstraction 1959-2015, Source: *Internet*

The CPS Ladder of Abstraction has its roots in the 1950s. Today numerous versions exist incorporating many refinements to the original logic.

Since the founding of Humantific, strategic challenge framing has been integrated into not only how we work with organizational leaders upstream from briefs, but how we think about and make sense of problem constellations. Challenge mapping is itself a form of upstream sensemaking. Often in real time with many constituents, present challenges are mapped from broadest at the top to narrowest at the bottom. This knowledge is rooted in CPS methods rather than in traditional downstream design methods.

Today working not from individual briefs (framed challenges), but rather in the context of challenge constellations is fundamental to numerous strategic design thinking practices. (See Who Owns How Might We?) This orientation differs significantly from the logic of traditional design, design thinking in both education and practice. Challenge maps are real-time versions of problem/challenge scale ladders.

Real-Time Open-Frame/Strategic Challenge Mapping, Source: *Humantific*

In terms of design as a subject, we of course knew that Professor Richard Buchanan, a highly respected design education scholar with a deep background in the subject of rhetoric, had tabled an ordering logic called Four Orders of Design in 1991.

Buchanan stated:
> *"Design is the human power of conceiving, planning and making products that serve human beings in the accomplishment of their individual and collective purposes..."*

> *"In approaching design from a rhetorical perspective, our hypothesis should be that all products – digital and analog, tangible and intangible - are vivid arguments about how we should lead our lives."*

> *"Products represent the formal causes, in the sense of the formal outcome of the design process that serves human beings."*

> *"The new design finds expression in rhetoric and dialectic."*

It was no secret that Buchanan's ordering framework was informed by rhetorician Richard McKeon's earlier four order model that suggested philosophic thinking is "manifested" in four ways as:

1. Personal Statement
2. Social Integration
3. Scientific Formulation
4. Insight Into Fundamental Values

Of course rhetoric ordering logics have been around for ages! McKeon's four-part rhetoric model was likely informed by numerous earlier works including Francis Bacon's (1561 –1626) three-part model: reason, imagination, will; Cicero's (106 BC) five canons of classical rhetoric: invention, arrangement, style, delivery, memory; Aristotle's (330ish BC) three-part rhetorical triangle ordering logic: logos, ethos, pathos, and; Plato's (460 BC) four-part rhetoric model: delivery, style, organization, content.

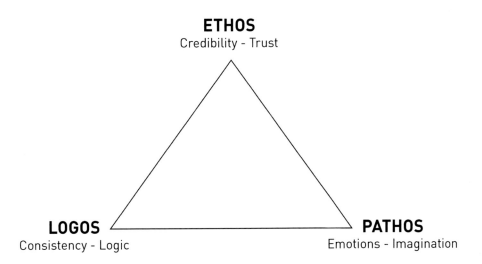

Aristotle's Three Part Rhetorical Triangle, Source: Internet

For Professor McKeon the notion that a type of thinking can be or is "manifest" in different ways evidently made sense in the context of depicting the shifting sands of rhetoric.

Importing the "manifesting" orientation Dr. Buchanan stated: "The four orders of design - manifested in symbols and images, physical artifacts, actions and activities, and environments or systems - represent new fields of cultural study as well as professional practice."

In Professor Buchanan's Four Orders of Design the manifestations were then mapped to the design discipline logic that existed at that time in 1991. The result is a two part combination manifesting/discipline picture.

1. Symbols (Symbolic and Visual Communications)
2. Things (Industrial Design/Material objects)
3. Action (Interaction Design/Activities and organized services)
4. Thought (Environmental Design/complex systems/environments for living, working, playing, learning)

From the outset, Four Orders of Design was depicted in the academic community as all encompassing, full-spectrum, and holistic.

While Professor Buchanan evidently found it useful, perhaps in a theoretical sense, to import the "manifesting" ordering orientation from the field of rhetoric, that three-part rationale of manifesting/discipline/full spectrum made little sense in the context of what our design community research revealed. Nor was it a fit with the spectrum of geographies that we knew from direct experience were already part of strategic design practice.

	Symbols	Things	Action	Thought
Symbols	Graphic Design			
Things		Industrial Design		
Action			Interaction Design	
Thought				Environmental Design

Design Issues: Volume 17, Number 4 Autumn 2001

Four Orders of Design, Source: *Richard Buchanan, 1991*

In addition and with all due respect, we found that the traditional design methodology described inside the framework of the 1991 Four Orders of Design presented a rather antiquated academic notion of how strategic design practices operate. The methodology described there focusing on a series of nested framed challenges is not representative of methodology being utilized in leading strategic design practices today.

Additionally, we noted the highest order application for design was depicted in the "Four Orders" model as "Environmental Design," as in designing the "environment/system" in which the designed activities and products reside. This is an "integrated product development" view of how design ecology works. Such views tend to be found in settings (schools and companies) with product design legacy orientation. This is not the orientation of leading strategic design practices today.

Even with the most generous interpretations of the terms "Action" and "Thought," such notions do not map to the geographies of organizational and societal challenges. Nor do Interaction Design challenges and Environmental Design challenges equate to diverse organizational challenges and diverse societal challenges. From our experience working with organizational leaders for years, we already knew that not all organizational challenges are product-related and not all involve interaction or the environment. The same applies to societal challenges.

The often cited supportive papers such as Tony Golsby Smith's 1996 paper, "Four Orders of Design: A Practical Perspective," mirrored the conceptual and methodological antiquation stating; "Design is the conceptualization and creation of products."

We saw that in academic circles three Case Studies were routinely cited when referencing Fourth Order Design. 1. Tax Forms Simplification Project, 2. DMM Transformation Project, 3. Australian Tax Office Project. Utilizing challenge framing logic, we could see that those case studies translate into these three relatively straightforward challenges:

1. How Might We redesign the US Postal Service's Domestic Mail Manual document?
2. How Might We simplify IRS tax forms?
3. How Might We teach the Australian Tax Office Design 2 (product creation) skills?

Not only were none of those challenges "wicked problems," but from todays practice perspective all of those are downstream-framed product design (Design 2.0) challenges, not upstream fuzzy organizational challenges (Design 3.0) or upstream fuzzy societal challenges (Design 4.0).

The picture painted by the academic literature related to "Four Orders" was not strong on methodology and conveys the misleading message that traditional design methods scale to full-spectrum challenges. As practice-based methodologists, we already knew this was not the case.

What we saw was that while the academic community often sought to split hairs over redefining what a product is, significant differences in methodology from scale to scale would routinely be denied, deflected, and ignored in favor of depiction that traditional design methods scale to all spectrums of challenges, as taught in numerous high profile graduate design schools.

Today in practice we know from a methods perspective that product, service, interaction, experience ,and environmental design all jump off from a framed challenge (brief) and thus are part of Design 2.0. Design Scale 3 is the operating zone where all kinds of organizational challenges exist, not just product, service, or experience challenges. Design 4.0 is the zone where extremely diverse societal challenges exist. From a methods perspective, Design 1.0 and Design 2.0 are downstream in nature, while Design 3.0 and Design 4.0 start in a different, upstream place.

To be brief, we concluded that contrary to much of the existing academic literature, the context, geography, scale, methods, framing, and logic of the 1991 Four Orders of Design model does not map to how or where strategic design practice operates today. There was a considerable misfit there. The "Four Orders" framework therefore was not practical to our sensemaking project.

Certainly we could see that Buchanan's underlying intention in 1991 was to point out that "We are in the middle of a revolution in design thinking..." It seems likely that Four Orders of Design reflected how the revolution must have looked from his scholarly, rather academic perspective in 1991. Since 24 years have passed, it is not so surprising that the next generation practice community is operating today in a rather different universe and with different methods.

The picture painted by the academic literature related to "Four Orders" was not strong on methodology and conveys the misleading message that traditional design methods scale to full-spectrum challenges.

Oddly, in addition what we saw during the research period was that the notion of "manifesting" as depicted in good faith by Professor Buchanan was being creatively, some might say defensively, re-de-picted. This was particularly true in the design education community as confirmation not only that de-signers already inherently had the skill to "manifest" across what was being depicted in "Four Orders" as full scale/full spectrum by magically shifting their brain focus, but that this level of skill was already embedded in graduate design education programs....meaning that the faculties already possessed such full spectrum skill and were actively teaching it.

It became evident that while this skills possession might have been true of the smaller 1991 universe depicted in "Four Orders," it was/is certainly not true of the broader terrain in play within organizational and societal transformation today. The research showed that the already magically manifesting at full scale/full spectrum depiction was a false narrative.

Whether intended by Buchanan or not, the magically manifesting school of thought seem to align more with the mythology of design as a form of magic thinking rather than with the actualities of the orientation, tools, methodology and skills indicated in the NextD research. In essence, there was no research, science, or evidence behind the design as magic thinking depictions. What we saw was that the false narrative of magic thinking was often being used to deflect what was from our perspective straight-forward problem finding and problem acknowledging related to methodology deficiencies in strategic design education today. Of course it was not difficult to see how Buchanan's foreshortened manifesting framing would be popular among the design education community, but the logic of mag-ically manifesting across full-spectrum was the opposite to our findings. This news upset numerous design education apple carts. Defuzzing and sensemaking can be difficult. :-)

Among our concerns was that while the design as magic thinking approach might serve the faculty political needs, it was tremendously unfair to a new generation of students seeking skills synchronized to a real changing world. It made sense that giving voice to that unfairness would prove to be part of the human-centered/user-centered NextD story.

To be fair to Dr. Buchanan, it seemed unlikely to us that he intended his 1991 framework to be cited for decades by slow-to-adapt design educators as a quasi rationale for why no meaningful strategic change was needed in design education.

While the political/defensive posturing by numerous design educators was unfortunate, counterproductive, and of no interest to us, it was clear that we needed a new-generation alternate framework, a reconceptualization that more closely reflected realities on the ground in the present-day context of strategic design practice.

As methodologists, we particularly wanted to offer more specifics in terms of how the complexity scale plays itself out from a challenge, skills, and methods perspective. This kind of focus and detail is not found in any of the existing "manifest" models.

For those so inclined, Dr. Buchanan's Four Orders of Design framework is still out there and we certainly recommend that anyone interested in the subject should read the papers from that period. (see examples below) If that logic and architecture makes sense to readers, they should go that route.

What we liked most about Buchanan's 1991 observations were these comments:

> "Design is a remarkably supple discipline, amenable to radically different interpretations in philosophy as well as practice."

> "The pluralism that is inherent in the ecology of culture will continue."

It was in this spirit and with no disrespect to any of the historical problem solving and/or design ecology models intended that we determined that a new hybrid ordering logic, acknowledging need for change, would best explain the findings and the challenges surfaced in the NextD research. This is where the NextD Geographies framework came from denoting the expanded/ reconstituted practice zones of Design Scale 1.0, 2.0, 3.0, 4.0 and the interconnected acknowledgment of the need for shift from magic thinking to skill-to-scale.

In NextD Geographies we are not mapping manifestations to discipline logic, but rather challenge scale logic to implications from a methods perspective. We combined the notion of a rising complexity scale with an increasing challenge scale and then interconnected it to methodology differences. NextD Geographies is challenge-scale-focused and assumes a multidisciplinary world. Once we had laid out the NextD Geographies framework it was not difficult to layer on the various findings. This was not just about acknowledging difference in challenge scale. Ultimately we identified a dozen method related shifts underway in practice and not yet present in design education. These included: Shift from tiny scale to large scale challenges, from low complexity to high complexity, from defined to fuzzy, from internalized process to externalized process, from downstream to upstream starting points; from tactical to strategic; from strangemaking

It became evident that while this skills possession might have been true of the smaller 1991 universe depicted in "Four Orders," it was/is certainly not true of the broader terrain in play within organizational and societal transformation today.

to sensemaking and changemaking; from thinking and doing to thinking, doing and enabling, from prescriptive to orchestrative, from intertribal communication to cross-disciplinary communication; from deliberate exclusion to deliberate inclusion; from magic thinking to skill-to-scale, etc. All of these insights were shared with thousands of NextD subscribers.

The orientation and skill change implications in Activity Emphasis Shift (page 34-35) alone, presented prior to the arrival of the big data era, will keep design educators busy for the next ten years. Add into the mix the Design Thinking Made Visible research that we undertook in parallel to the NextD Journal conversations and it became rather clear that much methodology renovation work needs to be done in design education.

To be brief, what all of that means is that Four Orders of Design and NextD Geographies not only depict significantly different universes but assume different methodologies and different skill sets, the former being narrower, less detailed, and less methodology-oriented than the later.

Most significantly NextD Geographies approaches community problem finding and problem acknowledging vastly different from how Four Orders of Design is being interpreted today. NextD Geographies steps up and bites the problem acknowledging bullet while Four Orders of Design has unfortunately been reduced to a change avoidance scheme. From our practice-based perspective, having diversity of sensemaking lenses for practitioners, educators, and other disciplines to make use of is positive and constructive.

A rough football analogy to the community research findings, sensemaking story would be a situation where the goal posts had been moved in the middle of a football game. We did not move the goal posts. The posts were moved by the marketplace. By 2005, the marketplace had moved the everyday challenges in which leading strategic design-oriented firms are now called upon to engage and are engaged.

The orientation and skill change implications in Activity Emphasis Shift alone, presented prior to the arrival of the big data era, will keep design educators busy for the next ten years.

Some educators seemed to be more aware of the shift than others. Some were very interested in engaging with us. Others insisted that the goal posts had not been moved. Some seemed to be offended that practice leaders were pointing this out. Some sought to remain in isolation on their academic discussion lists. Some academics continue to reference Four Orders of Design as an all encompassing, not-to-be-challenged holy grail. Many had been slow to adapt to the goal post/methodology changes. As a result some were downright hostile towards the message and the messengers. Some are just now finally acknowledging the goal posts movement. This is part of what has happened on the bumpy road between 2003 and today.

Adapting to the goal posts being moved in a timely way, the strategic design practice community had by 2005 already changed how we engage. The boundary assumptions and methodology assumptions from 1991 were already ancient history. The application of human-centered design at the scale of organizations and societies has been emerging and refining in the practice community not since last year, but rather for more than a decade.

Anyone missing that turn in the road would be having a difficult time really understanding what is going on in the design, design thinking community today.

Followers of NextD and/or Humantific have known of the goal post shifts and its methodology implications since 2005. We have been conducting public skill-building workshops since 2005. What the institution-based design education community has been doing is another story.

The key to understanding the various reactions to NextD Geographies is that it contains change drivers absent from the 1991 magically manifesting Four Orders of Design. NextD Geographies seeks to more clearly explain what is changing in the real world; in practice, what is present in design education as well as what's missing specifically from a methods perspective.

We learned a lot about our own community from the NextDesign Leadership sensemaking experience. Among other things what we found was that not everyone was ready for more clarity around this subject of design, design thinking, design education. Clarity and sensemaking are not the goals of everyone operating in a competitive marketplace, and that now includes the graduate design schools and their leaders responsible for timely adaptation leadership.

Most significantly, NextD Geographies approaches community problem finding and problem acknowledging vastly differently from how Four Orders of Design is being interpreted today.

As practice leaders seeking to hire design school graduates, it was often rather puzzling to see the defensive reaction from design education leaders to a call for change in the direction of strategic upskilling. What we found was that new-generation practitioners and students welcomed more clarity around the subject while older generation practitioners and educators found the clarity threatening to their traditional ways.

As sensemakers what we found was that cutting through the often heavily defended mythology around design education proved to be much more difficult than actually making sense of the research findings. To a large degree our community sensemaking made us outsiders to the myth-making neighborhoods of our own community.

The NextD story is not just about the goal posts moving. It also encompasses what to do about it from strategy, methods, skills, and leadership perspectives. It was and is a form of community leadership taking place by practice leaders without permission from institution-based design education leaders.

Today, NextD Geographies tends to be NOT the preferred sensemaking framework for those academic leaders still engaged in defensive posturing due to their own slow adaptation leadership, but that's OK with us. No big surprise there. Not everyone gets it at the same time.

As stories go, what turned out to matter most is understanding that the dawdling, slow motion adaptation of design education leaders did not slow the change taking place in strategic design practice community. All the deflection and slow motioning by design education leaders really did was delay meaningful strategic change in design education. Now much of that community is playing catch up. The practice community has since 2005 been steadily building knowledge of how to operate in these expanded terrains.

We have been consistent advocates of strategic change in design education since the creation of the NextD Geographies framework, first presented in 2005.

The good news is that an ever-increasing body of research and input from practice leaders continues to suggest significant design education change, alternate tracks are not just needed, but are now long overdue. It's not enough to rename product design programs "social innovation." :-) We have been consistent advocates of strategic change in design education since the creation of the NextD Geographies framework, first presented in 2005.

Since we were probably ten years out in front of the design education community when we started talking about this subject, what we see is that much of what we have been defuzzing for years is just now starting to be acknowledged in the design education community.

What is rather humorous is to see some of the same design education leaders who postured the magically manifesting mode for a decade now seeking to urgently reposition themselves as evidence experts and industry leaders in a movement being framed as "evidence-based design." For veterans of this arena, that's a real head spinner. It is absolutely necessary to have a sense of humor in this business. :-)

As practice leaders looking for new talent, we would certainly be happy to see more evidence-based design education!

Still today, a decade into the shifts described in NextD Geographies, we still see very few graduates coming out of the graduate/post-graduate design academies with upstream skills. Most graduate design programs remain focused on teaching Design 2 skills related to product, service, and experience creation. The strategic design practice community has long ago moved on.

Since launching NextD Geographies and the various interconnected models, we went on to complete the Design Thinking Made Visible Project (posted on Issuu as a virtual book) and the book, Innovation Methods Mapping: Demystifying 80+ Years of Innovation Process Design. Our focus on advancing methods-related knowledge continues.

Right now what we see is rising interest on the part of savvy organizational leaders seeking to cut through the fog that has increased substantially in the past few years around the subject of design/design thinking. As strategic design practitioners, we make use of NextD Geographies in all conversations related.

Without some kind of sensemaking framework linked to method and skill realities, making sense of the various claims and statements being made in reference to the subject of design thinking is virtually impossible. A lot of postings to blogs and online group conversations on the subject of design thinking takes place without such frameworks and tends to go around in endless circles.

Frankly speaking, we no longer bother with conversations where no sensemaking framework is present and/or where the magic thinking advocates are driving the train.

We are happy with our contribution to community sensemaking. Hundreds of readers access the NextD Futures Library every month on Issuu.

For some time we have redirected our attention to Humantific practice, working with organizational leaders, modeling the actualities within NextD Geographies and building our sensemaking/changemaking knowledge. We don't expend too much energy in the direction of online debating.

I appreciate you asking this question, Ana, and your patience with my detailed reply. We might need to add a few more parts to this conversation. :-)

Ana Barroso: One of the layers of findings you apply to the NextD Geographies framework has to do with the toolboxes that are increasingly more complex and cross disciplinary in Design 3 and 4. What skills does it take to conduct a visual sensemaking process? Do you believe a non-designer, without formal academic training, can make a good 3.0 or 4.0 design thinker or sensemaker? Can you describe the process of capacity building Humantific does in its innovation capacity programs?

GK VanPatter: Hi Ana. I see you like to ask difficult questions! OK I am happy to continue our conversation here. If our purpose is to quickly make sense of what is going on in strategic design practice today, ie: how we help others, several mind-shifts beyond traditional notions of what design thinking is and does are useful.

> Without some kind of sensemaking framework linked to method and skill realities, making sense of the various claims and statements being made in reference to the subject of design thinking is virtually impossible.

To a significant degree the practice of applying design thinking in the context of organizational and societal changemaking has already changed to the degree that it might be unrecognizable to some folks working in traditional design ways. This is one reason why we say design thinking is not one thing, but rather changes from scale to scale. That's not a future prediction. That's already a done deal. What's going on is less about transforming traditional design practice and more about creating new paths and new forms of practice. That train has already left the station, or perhaps more precisely, multiple trains.

Mainstream media still tends to depict the purpose of design thinking as product, service and experience creation. While those all remain very useful contributions that is a rather old-school, old-news approach to design thinking. It is a depiction that misses much of the frontier work going on today in the strategic design practice community.

In new practice design thinking there is already a more robust and realistic methods-oriented outlook. Part of that outlook shift is recognizing that to work openly and effectively in the organizational change (Design 3.0) and societal change (Design 4.0) requires a diverse toolbox that engages without preconceived assumptions regarding what the challenges are and what solution paths might be.

This is rather straight-forward logic, but in the fuzzy haze of old-school design thinking it was often lost in the spin. In new-practice design thinking, less spin and more clarity is already expected.

In complex organizations and societies, why would we assume that all challenges are product, service, and experience related and require product, service, and experience outcomes? In new-practice design thinking we make no such assumptions. One could think of this as practice or methodology innovation, but certainly this is among several significant shifts that leading strategic design practices have already made away from traditional design logic.

> In complex organizations and societies, why would we assume that all challenges are product, service, and experience related and require product, service, and experience outcomes?

The graduate design schools don't like to talk about it, but traditional methodologies that begin with pre-determined challenge and outcome path assumptions such as product, service, and experience design (Design 2) are not ideally suited for complex upstream strategic contexts. This remains a not-often-talked-about elephant in the old-school design thinking living room. In new-practice design thinking we talk openly about that elephant from a methods perspective. We are able to do that because we don't have legacy investment in Design 2 product/service/experience creation.

Regarding your question: "Do you believe a non-designer, without formal academic training, can make a good 3.0 or 4.0 design thinker or sensemaker?" I will take those as two different questions.

Lets do the sensemaking part first. At Humantific, we consider sensemaking to be part of the innovation process, the design thinking process, part of all design-related projects. In new-practice design thinking, sensemaking plays an increasingly significant role. As challenges grow more complex, more sensemaking is needed to get ready for changemaking. Making sense of fuzzy complexity (not just data analysis) is what sensemaking is all about. To keep it simple: Effective sensemaking can fuel innovation in a complex world. Making those connections in adaptable, sharable ways is already part of strategic design practice.

As a professional activity sensemaking involves a hybrid set of skills and for traditional design folks, a few mind-shifts. Making sense of something is not the same as making something different. Creative Intelligence pioneer WJJ Gordon famously referred to these two distinct activities as "sensemaking (making the strange familiar) and strangemaking (making the familiar strange)." This remains a useful construction. Object differencing (strangemaking) is deeply embedded in traditional design education and in all aspects of the branding/product creation business, making one bottle of water look different from another. Object differencing (strangemaking) has been the primary focus of many design programs for many decades.

While doing candidate interviews, we see many design school graduates with portfolios full of brand-related differencing (strangemaking) projects when we are looking for sensemakers. After ten years of making the suggestion, and with the help of the Big Data wave, the design schools are finally catching on to the need for more advanced sensemaking skills. It is no big secret that the graduate schools are often not synchronized with the many changes that have already taken place in strategic design practice.

Object differencing (strangemaking) has been the primary focus of many design programs for many decades.

Our Humantific version of Visual Sense-Making combines an innovation research orientation with advanced problem framing skills and deep information design skills. A key aspect is the underlying understanding-centered orientation described by our friend and sensemaking pioneer Richard Wurman, as: "Knowing what its like to not understand." This is a form of human-centeredness that not everyone has.

Since the graduate design schools are still not teaching what Humantific does, we tend to look for folks with natural tendencies towards sensemaking. These are often revealed in personal rather then curriculum projects.

Folks who have a natural inclination towards sensemaking, but not the formal information design skills tend to be best suited to the front-end of sensemaking. This initial activity has been referred to historically (by Marie Neurath of Isotype) as the "Transformer" role. The Transformer is a super analyzer and organizer of ordering systems working in the space between the mess and the formal information design capability. Ideally, Humantific wants folks who can do all aspects from analyzing and ordering to final visualizations that are then integrated directly into the changemaking process. This integration has always been at the heart of how we do what we do.

Humantific does teach basic Visual SenseMaking skills to organizational leaders from diverse backgrounds, and many find even introductory skills to be a powerful addition to their business-thinking toolbox. Not everyone is suited and equipped to become an advanced Visual SenseMaking practitioner, but even basic visual sensemaking skills can be a significant leadership value-add.

Since the 1980s, the American organizational theorist Karl Weick has written extensively on the subject of sensemaking and the need for organizations to do sensemaking on a continuous basis in a continuously changing world. In Weick's world there are no professional sensemakers but his views on organizational sensemaking remain very useful and important none the less.

What Humantific is doing is helping organizations formalize and supercharge that capability by bringing professional sensemaking skill, and skill-building. Among other things, we teach how formal sensemaking fits together with formal changemaking.

Since the 1980s, the American organizational theorist Karl Weick has written extensively on the subject of sensemaking and the need for organizations to do sensemaking on a continuous basis in a continuously changing world.

Regarding the other part of your difficult question: In Humantific-land design thinking is not a separate universe from design. We have noticed that some of the graduate business school leaders have been eager to pitch the rather self-serving narrative that design thinking is a separate logic since they are in need of reinventing themselves and seek to capture the upstream strategic work. Frankly speaking, that is more about competitive marketing and less about knowledge, skill, or marketplace realities. It's a view that discounts the reality that the strategic design practice community already exists and has existed for more than a decade.

Unfortunately we have seen that numerous design education leaders have laid down under that bus without understanding the implications. From our perspective, side-stepping responsibility for the leadership of our profession or transferring it to arriving others never made much sense. We do notice that most arriving armchair experts have foreshortened interpretations of design thinking in mind. Regardless of who might be strategically awake or asleep at any given moment, we certainly have no interest in surrendering to reduced notions of what is possible for the application of design/design thinking in business and in societies.

All considered, we do see a need for strategic design practice leaders to participate directly in the reinvention of and modeling of new practice design thinking beyond Design 2.0. Again this is not a future prediction, but at this point a work in progress, ten years in the making. For us it is just part of what we do without anyone's permission. No practice leader that I know is sitting around waiting for, or expecting, the academic institutions to figure out the future of strategic design practice.

Part of what makes your question complicated is that even recognizing that design thinking is in motion, there is a core orientation there that is important to know deeply. There are numerous avenues into that knowledge and awareness. Some avenues have more depth than others, and certainly different people have different needs. Much of that orientation cannot be mastered deeply by watching YouTube videos or reading books. Presently the graduate design schools still represent relatively deep embodiment of that basic human-centered orientation even if they are still teaching downstream Design 1.0 and Design 2.0 methodologies.

Practice-based skill-building programs, including our own Humantific Academy, tend to adapt more rapidly, are geared to mid-career professionals, and are already teaching next-generation open frame, strategic design thinking skills.

It might also help if we think of your question in terms of real-world practice, rather then hypothetical individual designers. You are correct in that the firms engaged in Design 3 and 4 tend to be multi-disciplinary assemblages of professionals from different backgrounds who contribute to the delivery of services being offered under the banners of design thinking or innovation. Are they all formally-trained design professionals? Often by design they are not.

In this regard it is important to appreciate that among the shifts in strategic design practices operating in the organizational and societal change space is the on-boarding of numerous activities not found in traditional design historically. One key activity is co-creation facilitation, a process, not content role. The NextD Geographies work pointed out that as challenges scale and involve many diverse stakeholders, much more cocreation facilitation will be and already is needed. Again, this is one of numerous method-related practice innovations or shifts that has already occurred in leading strategic design practices.

All considered, we do see a need for strategic design practice leaders to participate directly in the reinvention of and modeling of new practice design thinking beyond Design 2.0.

Senior people operating in this part of our Humantific practice may or may not come from design education backgrounds. As advisors, our practice requires extremely high levels of innovation methodology knowledge and facilitation skill. The truth is; Much of this knowledge is not found in the traditional design community. As far as we know there are no graduate design schools teaching co -creation facilitation skill at any depth. The only way to get there is to reach beyond traditional design approaches. We teach this skill, but most graduate schools do not.

Most strategic design practices on-boarded considerable methods knowledge from the Applied Creativity (Creative Intelligence, Creative Problem Solving, CPS) community a decade ago. The truth is most strategic design practices are at this point hybrid in nature and the skills being taken to market tend to be diverse. This is part of what makes your question complicated.

At the end of the day, the depth, timeliness, and flavor of any multidisciplinary innovation approach depends to a significant degree on the backgrounds and orientations of the founders and/or leaders of the company. Firms with engineers, scientists, or marketing experts leading them tend to frame, conceptualize, and deliver innovation-related services quite differently.

Humantific founders were educated in graduate design schools so this orientation is deeply embedded in everything we do, even while we on-board many other forms of knowledge from numerous other disciplines. We find that there is tremendous need for human-centered services, including culture building, so our approach is well suited to this expanded context.

Also important is to appreciate that Design 3.0 and Design 4.0 participants from diverse backgrounds are not typically creating toothbrushes, cars, or iPads. They are often grappling with complex, fuzzy organizational and societal challenges of many types.

Perhaps it might be helpful to some readers if I point out that underneath our day to day operations we tend to be constantly engaged in this five-part Humantific dance step:

- Being human-centered (also referred to as life-centered since humans are not the only beings on planet earth).
- Working directly with organizational leaders grappling with complex challenges, sharing knowledge and learning.
- Reinventing design/design thinking methodologies as challenges scale.
- Importing and adapting knowledge from other fields.
- Shifting from just doing project work to doing team-based capacity building and culture building.

One key to understanding what is going on in the next generation design practice community is to be aware that many traditional old-school design practices act methodologically as extensions of specific graduate school programs that have deep legacy roots in Design 1.0 or Design 2.0. Those firms tend to operate within the confines of Step 1 of the dance referenced above using traditional Design 1.0 or 2.0 methods. Those firms tend to be not so in sync with where the market expectations, challenges, and opportunities have shifted to.

Suffice it to say we are not intertwined with that picture. It is probably safe to say that no leading strategic design practice is a simple projection of what is going on in the graduate design school programs.

Our clients expect much more of us and we are not followers of any specific grad school manifesto. As a hybrid practice our goal is to truly be useful in diverse problematic contexts, not just product and service design. Our clients are organizational leaders and their needs have played a significant role in the development and fine tuning of what we do and how we do it. We design services from the outside in.

In terms of your capacity-building-related question: Close to 50% of our business is cross-disciplinary innovation skill-building, inclusive culture building, innovation capacity building. We work with many organizational leaders, not just doing projects, but creating innovation groups, centers of strategic design excellence, core teams inside organizations capable of driving change, building out their cultures, and working upstream from briefs.

What we are out in the world teaching to others, including organizational leaders from many backgrounds, is embodied in our Complexity Navigation Program which includes Strategic Co-Creation, Design Research and Visual SenseMaking. These are 21st century leadership skills.

In reference to generally what is changing in the new practice design thinking arena, as challenges scale up, we published, some years ago, these NextDesign Leadership Principles as part of the NextD Geographies work:

Leadership Principles: Open Frame Design Thinking/Doing

- Design Thinking methods tools and skills change according to challenge scale
- Upstream tools are different from downstream tools
- Clarify, externalize, visualize process
- Cocreation rises as challenges scale in complexity
- Think constructing assumption-free challenge constellations, not jumping from briefs
- Proportion of sensemaking rises as challenge complexity increases
- Data is just one of many possible sources of insight
- Co-Creation facilitation is a process role, not a content role
- Cognitive Inclusion maximizes diverse team brainpower
- Process mastery enables continuous adaptability
- Process knowledge outlasts content knowledge
- Be navigationally useful in every problematic context

Each of those principles requires some form of practice innovation or change from traditional forms of operating. We further shared how new strategic design practice is different in a conference talk entitled: The OTHER Design Thinking first presented at a design thinking conference in 2013.

Not every design thinking firm is up for that journey. That makes for a usefully diverse marketplace of choices for clients seeking various types of input. Suffice it to say, Humantific is on that changemaking road and has been for some time.

In closing, I will mention that one thing we do notice in the broader community is that for those strategic design practices doing this kind of work, finding a conference that reflects and relates to the work is difficult. We have tried several, but to date have not yet found one. We have thought about organizing such a conference ourselves, perhaps in collaboration with like-minded others. Its something we do consider from time to time. We certainly welcome conversations with other strategic design practitioners.

It is probably safe to say that no leading strategic design practice is a simple projection of what is going on in the graduate design school programs.

REFERENCES

Buchanan, Richard. *Design and the New Rhetoric, Philosophy and Rhetoric.* Design Issues, Vol. 34, No 3, 2001.

Buchanan, Richard. *Wicked Problems in Design Thinking.* Design Issues, Vol. VIII, Spring, 1992.

Buchanan, Richard. *Design Research and the New Learning.* Design Issues, Vol. 17, Autumn, 2001. Copyright 1991.

Golsby-Smith, Tony. *Fourth Order Design: A Practical Perspective.* Design Issues, Vol. 12, Spring 1996.

Humantific. *Design Thinking Made Visible Research.* 2001-2015.

Humantific. *Innovation Methods Mapping: De-Mystifying 80+ Years of Innovation Process Design.* 2016.

Humantific. *The OTHER Design Thinking.* 2013.

Junginger, Sabine. *A Different Role for Human-Centered Design Within Organizations.* School of Design Carnegie Mellon University, 2005.

NextD. *When [Old Design Thinking] LOVE is Not Enough.* 2013.

"Philosophy is not methodology"

GK VanPatter

Defining
Design Thinking

MIND THE METHODOLOGY GAP

GK VanPatter
CoFounder, Humantic, New York
CoFounder, NextDesign Leadership Network

Originally published in 2017

As 2017 comes to a close, what we see in the marketplace around the subject of Design Thinking is a lot of smoke and mirrors that have confused zillions of people. The design community itself has created much of the confusion and unfortunately clarity leadership from the direction of graduate design education in particular has been less then ideal. Many have conflated Design Thinking Philosophy with Design Thinking Methodology when in reality one is not the other.

Humantific seems to be among only a few practices stepping up to point out that Design Thinking cannot be defined philosophically as an open-aperture problem solving approach, often described as capable of tackling "wicked problems," if the actual present state methods are assumption-boxed, presuming/recognizing/addressing only product, service, and experience challenges and outcomes. That makes no sense at all.

It is no secret that many diverse challenges in organizations and in societies exist that have nothing to do with creating more products, services, or experiences. Any skilled methodologist can tell you that open-aperture methods and assumption-based methods are two different things. They have different starting points and different outcomes.

Truth be told; This is presently the #1 elephant in the Design Thinking living room and one that has caused massive confusion. The spinning and selling of philosophy as methodology, downstream methods as upstream methods, assumption-boxed methods as open-aperture methods amounts to a Design Thinking hocus-pocus. Once you become aware it is not difficult to spot the hocus-pocus when it appears, and it is now widespread.

The good news is that with organizational leaders becoming more knowledgeable, more savvy, the hocus-pocus Era of Design Thinking is winding down.

The good news is that with organizational leaders becoming more knowledgeable, more savvy, the hocus-pocus Era of Design Thinking is winding down. We are optimistic that a new Methodology Ethics Era is dawning.

As a practice, we are at Humantific, already embracing and living in that era.

DEFINITIONS

DOWNSTREAM IN ORIENTATION:

PRODUCT/SERVICE/EXPERIENCE DESIGN THINKING
[These methods often being marketed as "Design Thinking"]

Key Words:
Downstream, situational, iterative, human-centered, empathetic, nonlinear, insight creation, sensemaking, acceleration, creating, optimizing, products, services, experiences

1. Is a situational, iterative, nonlinear, holistic product/service/experience creation process.

2. Oriented towards a project team or teams creating products/services/experiences.

3. Begins with preconceived assumptions that the challenges or opportunities are product/service/experience-related and will be outcomes as well.

4. Begins downstream in product/service/experience Opportunity Challenge Definition Phase.

5. Most often begins with a predefined product/service/experience brief.

6. Contains empathetic research-focused on insight creation that informs the creation of products/services/experiences.

7. Recognizes product/service/experience challenges.

8. Might contain a high degree of empathetic visual sensemaking that shapes insights for accelerated digestion by all participants.

9. Most often contains no surfacing or orchestration of innovation behaviors.

10. Most often contains no surfacing and orchestration of cognitive thinking style preferences.

11. Like a hammer, screwdriver and wrench, each is applicable situationally to product, service or experience challenges.

12. Can serve as a useful toolkit/skillset in the pursuit of product/service/experience creation capacity building.

OPEN FRAME DESIGN THINKING

[Also known as Meta Design Thinking, Strategic Design Thinking and Adaptable Inquiry]

Key Words:
Upstream, meta, iterative, human-centered, empathetic, nonlinear, creating, optimizing, insight creation, design research, data/information fueled, visual sensemaking, challenge framing, focus on right challenge, acceleration, adaptive, inclusive

1. Is a meta, iterative, nonlinear, holistic, human-centered innovation process.

2. Is oriented towards multiple participant, cross-disciplinary cocreation.

3. Begins with no preconceived assumptions regarding what the challenges and opportunities are.

4. Begins upstream in the Opportunity Challenge Definition Phase.

5. Begins with a fuzzy situation to be defuzzed.

6. Contains empathetic research insight creation that informs challenge framing and opportunities for changemaking.

7. Recognizes that a constellation of diverse challenges likely exist simultaneously that can be visually mapped.

8. Contains a high degree of empathetic visual sensemaking that shapes insights for accelerated digestion by all participants.

9. Contains the surfacing and orchestration of participant innovation behaviors.

10. Contains the surfacing and orchestration of participant cognitive-thinking style preferences.

11. Like a Swiss army knife, is adaptive to various challenge types found in organizational and societal contexts.

12. Serves as human-centered, adaptive toolkit/skillset in the pursuit of organizational adaptive capacity building.

Methodology
Ethics

EMBRACING THE NEW ERA

GK VanPatter
CoFounder, Humantific, New York
CoFounder, NextDesign Leadership Network

Originally published in 2017

While reading a recent thread posted by someone in one of the LinkedIn Design Thinking groups on the topic of industry ethics, I started to write a few comments on this always difficult subject. The tiny "comments" box was too small for my text, so I will make this into a brief blog post here. Yes, somewhat by this accident I started writing about a subject that has been percolating in the back of my mind for some time. It is something that occurred to us when we were working on our recently published book "Innovation Methods Mapping: Demystifying 80+ Years of Innovation Process Design."

The topic of community ethics is a rather dry but important one and I was somewhat surprised by the focus of that Design Thinking group thread in which these questions were initially asked: "What is the ethical grounding of design and design thinking? This includes what work one chooses to do as well as how one approaches the actual design. Are designers responsible for the ethics of their [output] designs?"

Appearing in that very interesting and lengthy, multiple participant conversation was the statement that "ethics is completely about being responsible" as well as concern being expressed regarding:

- Ensuring positive social impact
- Misusing empathetic research
- Negligence in security involving user information
- Bias in artificial intelligence
- Plutocracy worshipping
- Insincere adoption of human centered design
- Living in a Ponzi Scheme
- Avoiding exploitation of nature and society
- Data rights
- The values of a winner take all society
- Need for moral integrity

Also pointed out was the noble goal of "living an ethical life" and the suggestion that design thinking is "uniquely placed as a likely vehicle for a more ethical approach."

The thread ended with a participant pointing out that "the principles of respect, responsibility, and honesty are equally applicable to other stages of the design process [not just design research]."

I was surprised to see that missing from the lengthy discussion was one of the most important elephants presently in the design thinking living room, albeit difficult to get at and even trickier to talk about. It takes a methodology-oriented set of glasses to see it. Once you become aware you see it everywhere! Framed as an ethics issue it looks something like this:

Hidden in plain sight, a key ethics issue presently facing the design/design thinking communities, including the design education community, is widespread "creative" misrepresentation of methods and their predicted outcomes.

With the rise of interest in the subject of design thinking, the methodology redepiction phenomenon has skyrocketed. Whether it has risen to the point of becoming an industry ethical problem and whether or not anything can or should be done about it are among the debatable issues.

To any professional ethics-oriented body, the redepiction wave would raise several seldom-asked questions including:

When does creative marketing become unethical misrepresentation?

What are the reasonable responsibilities towards representation inherent in the professional practice of design/design thinking in its various forms?

Today, are there any articulatable ethical responsibilities for practitioners or is the practice of design/design thinking now a 100% wild west, take-no-prisoners, free-for-all?

WHAT'S THE NOT SO GOOD NEWS?

Presently, in the completely unregulated design/design thinking industries, there is really no such ethics oriented body as in a professional association of any significance.

For those who are new to the subject and might not know, historically many basic ethics and protocol standards came from and were taught in professional design schools.

Unfortunately much of that orientation has disappeared with the simultaneous repositioning of many graduate schools as revenue-generating consultancies. Out the window went the historical orientation to ethics and in its place the free for-all-dynamics of the competitive marketplace were imported.

Many graduate design schools now compete in the marketplace directly with their own graduates, often without any acknowledgment, formal study, research, or knowledge of consequences beyond generating revenue. A valuable ethics-centered community resource has been seriously compromised, eroded and largely lost in the often unacknowledged conversion of graduate design schools to revenue-generating businesses. In effect, the graduate design schools have eliminated themselves from the ethical guidance equation.

Facing the external world shift towards increased complexity of challenges in organizations and the planet, but slow to adapt at the R&D methodology reinvention level, most of the graduate design schools instead adopted the more marketing-oriented, rapid response notion of selling philosophy as methodology. It's a much faster adaptation fix then actually rethinking methods and related programs.

Today often broad world-peace-size, philosophical-transformation intention statements are routinely made but then without batting an eyelash oddly coupled with downstream assumption-boxed methods (Product/Service/Experience Design) being redepicted as upstream and universal. Not quite a bait-and-switch it is often more akin to design thinking hocus-pocus, a shell-game of sorts.

This phenomenon is now so widespread among the graduate design schools and many of their graduates that it has become the de facto industry standard. In conversation after conversation, right here on LinkedIn, one can see many arriving participants taking the philosophy as methodology hocus-pocus phenomenon for granted.

Unknown to eager incoming students, many graduate design schools are engaged in depicting and selling what they surely must know to be downstream assumption-boxed methods (Product/Service/Experience Design) as upstream open-aperture universal meta (Design Thinking) methods.

As those students eventually graduate and enter the real-world marketplace, their methodology indoctrination and disorientation often becomes evident, but the disconnect does not seem to concern the design schools from which they just exited. It's a subject that many in design academia would prefer not to talk about.

Unfortunately, as the popularity of design thinking grew, many of the relatively unenlightened business schools seeking to enter the same revenue-generating arena have adopted the hocus-pocus approach. Several versions of the downstream is upstream spin now exist, some more strategic than others.

Outside of academia in the parallel universe of business, unknown to many seeking Design Thinking services, numerous consulting firms are echoing what the graduate schools are modeling and doing. Many are knowingly engaged in depicting and selling legacy downstream, assumption-based methods (Product/Service/Experience Design) as upstream open-aperture universal meta (Design Thinking) methods.

Signing up for the redepiction hocus-pocus has become part of the procedural litmus-test indoctrination around the subject of design thinking often framed as: "Do you get it?" and "Are you a believer?"

Historically, many basic ethics and protocol standards came from and were taught in professional design schools.

As the teaching of skills being framed as "Design Thinking" become more and more dispersed into other disciplines with other value systems, there is no real center of gravity for ethical considerations. The bare-knuckle ethics and lack there of in the competitive marketplace now rule the roost around this subject.

Whether we all like it or not, it is that methods hocus-pocus that has become the #1 shell-game going on in the industry at the moment with many in the arena now involved including the highest profile American graduate design schools. Without doubt, it's a game that bumps directly up against numerous ethical questions.

Clearly this is a difficult subject and even raising it as a topic tends to generate heat. With heavy investments made in the selling of downstream as upstream, many would prefer that the subject never comes up, that the elephant, visible in plain sight, is never referred to or acknowledged.

WHAT'S THE GOOD NEWS?

What is (hopefully) coming is the end of the philosophy/methodology hocus-pocus era and a new era of Methodology Ethics. What's needed is a new era of heightened methodology awareness, transparency, honesty, ethics, and authentic reinvention.

As clients become more methodologically-enlightened, this is bound to occur one way or another. In the face of that enlightenment, many of the "creative" hocus-pocus redepictions presently flooding the marketplace will eventually fall away. In their place will be more honesty regarding the limitations of legacy, assumption-based methods.

The magic-thinking notion that traditional design methods scale to all contexts from toothbrush creation, to organizational transformation, to world peace, will give way to new and more enlightened calibration in the industry. The depicting of downstream methods as upstream methods will give way to more honest depictions and more meaningful choice. The graduate design schools will wake up to the challenge of making real methodology and program changes not fixable by tweaking marketing campaigns.

What is (hopefully) coming is the end of the philosophy/methodology hocus-pocus era and a new era of Methodology Ethics.

Most importantly, many new streams of creation around new approaches geared to broader more complex contexts will emerge. This stream is already underway.

Unfortunately, the present community leadership picture around this elephant in the design thinking living room is not great, and this makes for difficult problem recognition, acknowledgment, and changemaking.

At the moment, there seems to be no professional association-type bodies capable of weighing in on the subject, such as suggesting or setting ethical standards. With many of the graduate design schools up to their eye balls in the spin, it is unrealistic to expect any kind of meaningful leadership around this issue from that direction either. On top of all that, there is no real formal strategic design journalism or "press" to speak of, so the issue is unlikely to surface from that direction. Combined, it's a bit of a perfectly dysfunctional community storm.

This is not a problem that our practice owns, but as practitioners we can certainly recognize that it exists and is it having significant impact. The shell game itself has caused massive confusion around the subject among the public. It seems likely that if the hocus-pocus, issue is not somehow addressed, the design thinking era will likely be foreshortened, eclipsed, and or not fully realized.

At the end of the day, in spite of the community leadership void, we all decide consciously or uncon- sciously to place ourselves and our practices on one side or another of this issue. As practice leaders, we have, at Humantific, already made our choice.

It will surely be interesting to see how each side plays itself out going forward. As with most emerg- ing-change eras, this one is overdue and bound to be a bumpy ride. Clearly not everyone is ready.

Imagine yourself in a meeting and someone says something like this: "Design Thinking is an upstream process that helps take a new stance on a problem which old methods no longer solve." It is a true statement, but watch out for the hocus-pocus. What you want to do is ask: "Is that the philosophy or the methodology or both?"

If the Design Thinking they are talking about is "an upstream process," then the methodology can't be downstream, assumption-based product, service, or experience design. If you see broad upstream statements combined with downstream methods, then you know you are in the Design Thinking hocus-pocus Zone.

Is that hocus-pocus ethical?

You decide. Good luck to all.

Methodology House on Fire?

URGENCY IN METHODS REDESIGN

IN CONVERSATION

GK VanPatter
CoFounder, Humantific, New York
CoFounder, NextDesign Leadership Network

Peter Jones, PhD
Redesign Network
Associate Professor, Strategic Foresight and Innovation, OCAD University
CoFounder, Systemic Design Association, RSD Symposium

GK VanPatter: Hi Peter; This is our last conversation in this series and we have not spoken in a while, so lets do our best to restart this sensemaking engine between us one more time. :-)

As you will recall, it was around 2005 (wow, time flies by!) that you and I began pointing out the need for a new generation of design/design thinking/design doing methodologies.

To be specific, we pointed out the inadequacy of presuming that designerly assumption-boxed methods geared for product, service, and experience creation automatically apply to complex organizational and societal contexts. We framed the present mode of many crossing with their product, service experience methods and toolboxes into the arena of high complexity the "Cross-Over Era."

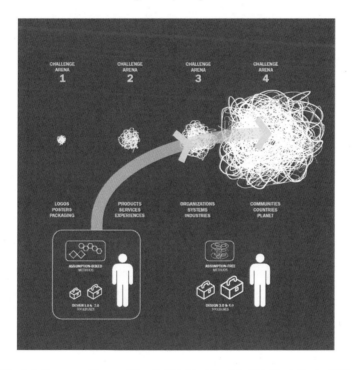

Cross-Over Era Model, Source: *Humantific, ReThinking Design Thinking, Page 139*

In the marketplace some got that, some did not. Many of our readers who did get it benefited from that sharing and are still with us. Others are just now coming around to many of the realizations that we were pointing out then regarding shortcomings of existing design-related methods.

As a prologue to this ReThinking Design Thinking book, I thought we might touch base and fold in a last round on some shifting sands that I have been reflecting upon recently. I have a feeling that this might be something that you have reflected upon for better or for worse, yourself Peter. That topic is urgency.

One would have to be asleep to be missing that as a new generation of folks arrive, expectations around changemaking and recognition of need for change in particular are shifting at breakneck speed finally.

While a new generation has very different notions regarding problem recognition, it seems clear that many of our changemaking processes, especially those that have roots in design, are not up to the task facing communities, societies, and the planet.

Examples of the shift in problem recognition and acceptance abound, but here are three that I can think off the top of my head:

Greta Thunberg: In 2018, the young Swede, Greta Thunberg, turned heads when, at 15 years of age, she articulated in a climate conference address a stunning perspective on the present generation of adults (all of us) that probably represents the views of many. In a form of reverse mentoring, Greta suggested: "You [present day adults] are not mature enough to tell it like it is. Even that burden you leave to us children." No question this generation is arriving with very different perspectives on the mess they see in front of them. Whether everyone likes it or not, whether everyone is ready for it or not, a new arriving generation is going to insist on the RAPID rethinking of those blockages, in the context of what they are beginning to perceive as their burning house.

UK and Irish Parliaments: The UK and Irish Parliaments declare climate emergency with protestors shouting "The Dinosaurs Thought They Had Time Too" :

Venice Biennale: Even the 2019 Venice Biennale was depicted as "Preaching to the Converted" as many exhibits were seen sounding the siren song of societal emergencies.

Thinking about this picture from a methodology perspective, clearly many of the societal challenges being pointed to are highly complex and far beyond the domains of product, service, and experience design methods.

With all of that in mind, let's start with this: From your perspective, are you seeing a new sense of problem recognition and urgency? What do you think are its implications for the design community?

Peter Jones: With respect to the pressure for urgent responses to complex problem systems, I'm seeing an enormous social dialectic playing out. A larger number of people are now demanding action to deal with the New Climate Regime (as Latour calls it). But there are several dialectics or conflicts that render conventional problem solving and deliberation approaches almost pointless. For what social purpose do we actually design when movements become entailed into politics and policies? The implementation of environmental values will differ extremely between indigenous rights-seeking groups in Canada and EU policymakers. The design implementation of affordable urbanism will become problematic, as we cannot easily undo 50 years of neoliberalism – not within the methods of design workshops at any rate. So methodology, appropriate to the problem scale and complexity, will become incredibly important.

As Latour also points out in this short 2018 book, the question of "what to do for climate action" is contested between strongly opposed frames of legitimate political stances. The old political frame of Left (Socialist or Progressive) through the "center" to Right (Conservative or Authoritarian) has been overworked by media and pundits since the Brexit and Trump transitions. As we see manufactured urgency by politicians who are rapidly losing tenure, they are doubling down on an old frame that complex problems have totally ignored.

Nature doesn't care what side you're on. But it might care about the truly urgent political frame of Globalization (which is now eroding), Nationalism, Regionalism, and Localism. Globalism

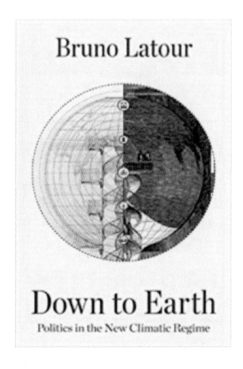

is very hard on natural resources, and regional/local policies tend to be restorative. However, much of the fuss at the policy level (including Greta's global march) has been instigated with globalist assumptions.

The West is splitting between globalization (which arguably contributed significantly to the environmental crisis) and the desire for relocalization, and anti-globalization (animated by the French Gilets Jaunes, for example). We can also locate the "strange attractor" of the U.S. election of President Trump between these, an outcome that has further divided some constituencies (e.g., environmental restoration activists and the rural renewal community) that ought to be aligning.

Generational theory suggests we really would be fighting in the streets by now, which we are (literally) seeing in cities in the US and UK.

We now face another complicating dynamic, the dialectic (either/or/both) of the demand for action for the earth "right now" vs. long-term strategies with responsible stakeholders. The introduction of the civic "climate emergency" has created pressure for responsive public optics, and the passing of these measures has not led to better policymaking, as the funding and deliberation have not followed. In fact, we can already see that climate emergencies create the conditions where serious planning might be scrapped in favor of immediate political busy actions that appear to be responsive to demands, but will ultimately fail without having an approach guaranteed by the participation of community stakeholders.

Many systems thinkers would share my concern that taking action on behalf of communities, yet without engaging stakeholder participation, is patently unethical and anti-systemic. This is my core issue with "urgency." Urgency only focuses the mind when your life is in immediate danger. It erodes the careful reasoning essential to collective decision-making otherwise. It leads to sloppy methodology and bad decisions that people go along with because they do not wish to be perceived as getting in the way of collective action (especially if it's a mob).

Although we have placed more emphasis on climate disruption effects recently, the sources of the environmental crisis were defined - and more urgently than now - in 1970 with the Club of Rome's continuous critical problems (and Limits to Growth) as well as the optimistic establishment of the environmental laws and the EPA.

The long crisis, taking shape in the geological frame of the Anthropocene, has been with us over a period crossing four generations. There have been shifts in these generations, with break points where new crisis conditions emerge and align (sometimes called turnings). The Greta generation (called Z, after X and Y) has spoken up earlier than usual in such a turning. Regardless of how many are in titular agreement, new activism creates the backdrop for huge inter-generational collision, not alignment.

However different generations also act on the issues handed to them as they come of age. Generational theory suggests we really would be fighting in the streets by now, which we are (literally) seeing in cities in the US and UK. And if you look around to other countries you will see signs of action on urgency. If you follow the French Yellow Vests, who have flooded the streets across most French cities every week for eight months now, you will notice they get no media attention. There is in this case inconvenient urgency that threatens powers that be, and false urgency that power can use.

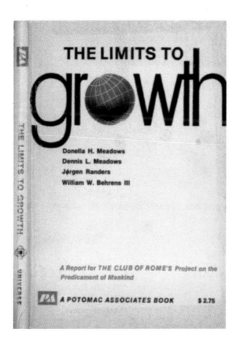

COLLISION OF VALUES

This collision of values and priorities necessitates a very different approach to social and systemic design than in previous eras. Our stances and methods have to enable legitimate, local deliberative democracy to yield consensus on action and high-quality planning. In my view (shared by others seeking to resolve these dilemmas), the ecological unit of planning and site of social action is the bioregion, not the nation-state. National policies can enable and fund regional programs, but they should not usurp the localized actions and developmental work needed to sustain human-ecological balance in real places.

I see our situation not in terms of specific policy issues such as climate change or media disinformation, but as civilizational. The urgency should be directed to recovering access to democratic means so that we can decide our courses of action in significantly better designed forms of consultation and deliberation as peoples who actually share a common civilization.

We [humans] have a very poor track record on attempting collectivist problem-solving when we have no functional means of reaching agreement on action. I think we must figure out the right things to do, and then act on the high-leverage proposals on which we can agree to invest. Acting under the time-generated moral pressure of a start-up movement is not the way to organize right action.

I'm glad there's interest in "doing something," but the pressure is being put on to leaders of dysfunctional governments. It will instead lead to actions taken to satisfy public pressure, which, given 21st century politics, is not rational. Instead, I think the burden of climate ecology action must be placed on our largest institutions that generate the highest impact - the military, government and defense contractors, global-spanning enterprises, banks, and government actors themselves. These actors require a different problem framing than policymakers, who are generally more focused on regulation and taxation.

> We [humans] have a very poor track record on attempting collectivist problem-solving when we have no functional means of reaching agreement on action.

I've worked with all these sides. As a professor and innovation researcher, I'm also involved in Canada's ecologizing (climate) movement, which I've observed to be more mature than the US, and maybe even a decade ahead. I co-founded the Drawdown Toronto program and brought it into OCAD University to connect with students and to engage the broader community in environmental solutions based on the known science. I co-founded the Flourishing Enterprise Institute which we launched this year as an international network of business innovation thinkers creating new methodologies for leading business to flourishing, what sustainability must sustain, at ecological, economic, enterprise and social levels.

LIFE-CHANGING AUDACITY

If I'm going to teach in a foresight program, it helps to act with life-changing audacity on one's own foresight. This takes skin in the game (willing to risk my future on my own insights). At least it makes a great story. Many people know my story, as do you, of a few years after my Ph.D. becoming an accidental election-reform activist when the 2004 election was defrauded by Ohio's Bush re-elect team. We moved the design firm to Toronto on foresight that the next decade or so would be extraordinarily better there than the US.

I teach systems thinking and futures methods and theory at OCADU's MDes programs. I believe that systems thinking and the approach we call Systemic Design are necessary to make sense of probable futures. If we merely position our desired future outcomes into space-time without an understanding of how social and cultural forces interact, we risk losing time and credibility, and failing in our desired social change. We have to articulate and disentangle the social systems and relationships that cycle forward into our futures. Systemic design is a way of doing this. As design scholars, practitioners, and educators, we have to better address the means and access to problem framing, and joint discovery of deep-rooted causes. It is not enough to know the technological solutions or to hold civic engagements for public education, we have to build agreement on best stakeholder actions, and to collaborate with those actors in system-level design programs. These are systemic design functions.

With all of that said, acknowledging that many of us are probably working on methods for new forms of "multi-stakeholder social transformation."

OCAD, Toronto, Canada, Source: *Internet*

DINOSAURS FALL

If urgency is about action, the dinosaur's fall to the nuclear winter of a meteor strike yields instead more fatalism. In my view, the prevention of the dinosaur's outcome should be planetary outrage at the US's insouciant dismissal of nuclear weapons treaties established from the last Cold War. President Kennedy attempted to draw down nuclear WMDs with the Soviet Union in 1961. We have lived with universal existential angst since then as the business model of the military-industrial-media complex has prevailed since then.

A real nuclear winter is something we can prevent right now. But the contrast between acceptable urgent issues (greenhouse gas emissions) and politically-ignored urgent issues (nuclear weapons, with broken treaties this year) is a classical study in social groupthink. We can all "actually" die from a nuclear mishap. We will "actually" die early if our healthcare system fails to support the changing needs of an aging population. And yet these are also issues we ought to be reframing in order to address their relevance, value to society, and astonishing expense.

Why don't we make a McLuhan Tetrad (a system-framing technique used in media ecology). What does urgency facilitate? What does it resolve to when pushed to extreme? What traditions does it now make present, and what does it obsolete? I will answer this in further discussion as we integrate our ideas. In the quick sketch of this, if we consider urgency a driver comprising the ground in which the raw expression of (for example) XR's climate marches are a figure, I might reveal in the outline why I'm feeling a bit like the foresight-based visioning and community design-planning we're doing is subjected to disruptions that might upend the beneficial outcomes of methodology.

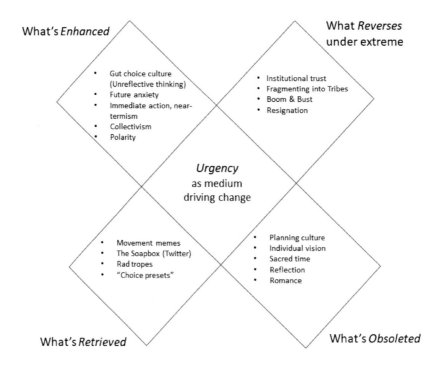

Source: Peter Jones: *OCAD*

- What's enhanced by Urgency: Unreflective thinking (Kahneman's System 1), Future anxiety, Near-termism, Collectivism
- What's Obsoleted (lower right): Planning culture, Individual vision, Sacred time, Reflection, Romance
- What's Retrieved (from the past eras): Movement memes, The Soapbox (Twitter), Rad tropes, Choice presets
- What Reverses (when pushed to extreme): Institutional trust, Fragmenting into Tribes, Resignation

And we can take a (Henry Dreyfus) MAYA approach, the "most advanced yet acceptable" solutions in climate action, which happen to be sociotechnical system changes we need to do anyway - energy transition, relocalizing food sources and reducing food waste, bioregion restorations, strict handling of refrigerants. A sane plan of action takes stakeholder engagement and advanced design planning. Are we doing that?

When people collectively become urgent, it is already too late to act on urgency. We make huge mistakes when acting under pressure and under the visibility of public optics. We do things that look good, such as "climate emergencies" when we (collectively) have no idea how to follow those up. And I speak as someone who in involved professionally with community and municipality-level climate-change action planning. It takes time and collaborative discourse to construct a community plan. To just act under pressure leads to irreversible mistakes, because we can never admit that we chose the wrong path.

GK VanPatter: It's true that Greta Thunberg has cynically been referred to as the Kim Kardashian of climate change but to go that route undervalues what is going on there I think. Greta is representational of a generation that is for better or worse behaving towards societal problem acceptance very differently from previous generations. In simple direct terms she suggests that the planet does not belong to the boomers. She directly suggests that the boomers have done an incredibly poor job of problem acceptance.

Of course the media platforms available now are much more pervasive then in previous eras where concerns were raised in various neighborhoods, but struggled to become broadly visible. In many ways Greta's performance on the world stage has been a global shout-out, wake-up call. I would even say a total shock for many boomers, accustomed to their old assumptions, those in power in particular. It does seem likely that more than a few noses have been knocked out of joint by the attention Greta has attracted to issues previously noted by others in previous generations, and perhaps in more detail, but lets not let that hold us back from recognizing the opportunities around the energy that the Greta crowd is generating and the need that is being pointing out.

Clearly Greta is not a methodologist, but there are methodology implications to what is being pointed out. I believe Greta is primarily engaging in problem finding and in particular enhancing problem acceptance among older generations, not solution generation. Unlike previous approaches, she is bound and determined to get the older generation to take responsibility for the mess that has been created. What she is doing there is kind of a reverse mentoring thing. Personally, I do not find that offensive, especially since her generation will shorty own these problems.

Acknowledging what others have pointed out previously including your colleagues in the Club of Rome, for the purposes of this conversation let's at least acknowledge that the alarm bells around large scale societal challenges are in the public realm sounding loudly right now.

Let's be clear that the challenge and opportunity for us here in this conversation is not to focus on Greta, Club of Rome documents, or even the climate problem in particular. Our NextD focus is not on any particular complex challenge, but rather on recognizing increasing complexity and need for thoughtful methods that synchronize with challenge scale.

The question is: Will Greta's energy be enough to light a fire under the design academies to recognize need for methodology change for that scale of complex challenges?

Earlier in NextD history we called this recognition Skill-to-Scale. We already know that mountains of complexity exist both at the scale of organizational changemaking and societal changemaking that are very different from product, service, experience complexities and assumptions.

Source: Internet

MAGIC THINKING vs SKILL-TO-SCALE

Perhaps for some readers just now joining the conversation it's important to reiterate that we have been doing this pointing out in the face of the wide spread notion (which still dominates much of the graduate design education industry) that design is a form of Magic Thinking, magically scalable in its most basic intuitive form to any challenge scale. Interconnected in design education today is the widespread selling of design philosophy as methodology.

Magic Thinking and Skill-to-Scale remain two polar opposite perspectives on the possibilities and realities of design. The former does not acknowledge need for change, while the later specifically calls for it.

Ten plus years out from when we first tabled concern in that direction, I still see much of the graduate design education community engaged in narrative warfare selling product/service/experience design methods, now repackaged as universal Design Thinking. In the marketplace there are multiple generations of folks who have been thus indoctrinated and sold that bill of methodology goods by the design academies. Some have PhD's walking around with this indoctrinated narrative.

You and I both know that repackaging design as Design Thinking did nothing to make those methods more strategic. In fact, it would not be difficult to make the case that the popularity of the Design Thinking movement while being utilized to drive change in other communities, including the business community and the business education community, has ironically largely served as a blockage for meaningful methodology evolution in much of the design education community in particular.

> Magic Thinking and Skill-to-Scale remain two polar opposite perspectives on the possibilities and realities of design.

OUR PURPOSE HERE

As we begin landing this plane in this last chapter, with the alarm bells sounding loud and clear in the public realm that attention to large-scale challenges are now needed, our purpose here is to turn to a few straightforward questions and to rearticulate our views as clearly as possible for readers.

A. Is the "Cross-Over Era STILL persistent? Is there STILL a gap between the scale of complex challenges needing attention asap on planet earth and the methods now connected to the subject of "Design" or "Design Thinking"?

B. Is the design community, including graduate and post-graduate design education really prepared from a methods perspective to engage around highly complex challenges beyond product, service, and experience assumptions?

C. Can the rapidly-emerging energy around solutions urgency be translated into recognition of the methods gap and needs for methods redesign within the design community, and design education in particular?

I will turn now to you, Peter, and invite you share your updated 2019 take on these issues before we look at one last question in this series.

Peter Jones: Regarding readiness: I would not characterize the general academic design community as methodologically ready for the scale of challenges and the urgency being referred to here.

The hard truth is that what we earlier identified as Design 4.0 societal-scale changemaking represents a huge shift in challenge scale for which design studies and literature show very little experience and success.

Regarding the question of forward motion and whether a fire can be lit under graduate design education I can only tell you what we are doing and we are already on fire!

As you know, a small band of Design 4.0 thinkers, including Birger Sevaldson, Harold Nelson and myself started the RSD Symposium initiative in 2011. We were concerned about the lack of designing power sufficient to emerging complexity. We had urgent ideas about mixed and hybrid methodologies, and we all promoted systems thinking approaches.

Regarding the question of forward motion and whether a fire can be lit under graduate design education, I can only tell you what we are doing and we are already on fire!

One of the purposes of this "movement" (if I might call it that) was and is to reconsider the power of design methods to better connect designerly methods to large-scale, complex fuzzy situations. We have for some time been quietly working on the Methods Gap. We have organized a yearly knowledge-sharing conference, and the work being framed as Systemic Design is ongoing though rigorous publications, dozens of cases shared in communities of practice, and hybrid methods in innumerable creative contexts.

We recognized the need for industrial strength methodologies for complexity contexts, and have been adapting systems methods with designerly forms. The venerable rich picture from Soft Systems has been exposed into the super-complex Gigamap and the visual narrative of synthesis mapping. We are adapting Christakis, Banathy, and Özbekhan's social systems design to fit today's multi-stakeholder engagements in public planning and organizational arenas. Latour's Actor Network Theory becomes embedded in modern workshop methods, as well as his Modes of Existence for stakeholder discovery. There is a full-lifecycle Systemic Design Toolkit co-designed with the leading Belgian design firm Namahn. The RSD proceedings and annual She Ji theme journals are building this repertoire.

We have been attempting to hybridize and reframe these methods for just such "matters of concern."

If I may include a diagram I use in teaching to demonstrate the range of systemic design methods we introduce (some of which we in OCAD University's MDes Strategic Foresight and Innovation), arranged by four intentions, all of which are often used in a project, but at different stages. The methods are color-coded by type.

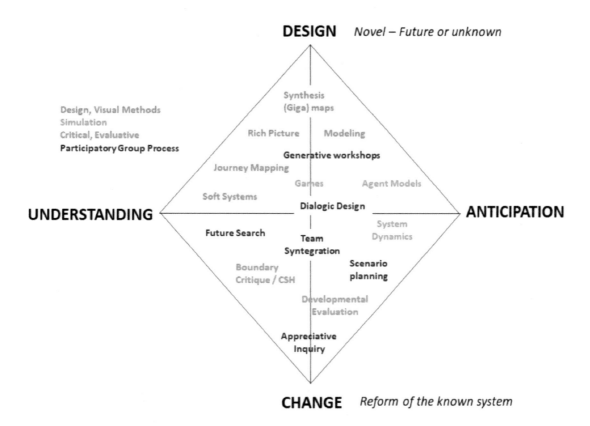

Four Intentions Framework, Source: Peter Jones: OCAD

I use a similar mapping to distinguish innovation research methods and for strategic foresight. What we teach besides a set of core methods - and that I believe cannot be taught remotely - are the contexts, guidelines, and heuristics for method selection and progression that best fit the problem/challenge design opportunity.

People often ask whether you can work on all these intentions at once. In research, these are separate stages of a complex project. Before engaging in anticipatory foresight work, it will be helpful to learn about the stakeholder environments and understand human culture and needs. Social change can be enabled by design, and of course there are organizational change demands required in major product/service transformations. But again, these are separate modes of research, with different research questions and methods.

I use Özbekhan's dilemma as one of the first provocations in our Systemic Design course, to unlearn problem solving. We have trained designers that their role and goal is to be problem solvers, based on four generations of design methods and philosophy that have evolved this perspective. You cannot expect to resolve complex challenges at the level of complex systems by applying problem-solving methods or the "solving" mindset.

I think what is happening here is that even between the two of us, significant differences remain even after we acknowledge the existing methods gap and need for change.

The problem-solving mindset is one of reductionism - fitting the situation into our perceptions as understood during a particular time and context. Social complexity develops and emerges over long periods of time, and the escalation and evolution of multicausal concerns (such as disruptive climate effects) are not unwound by problem - solving approaches. What's needed is creative argumentation across multiple perspectives, experts, stakeholders, and those less-powerful participants who are vulnerable to a bad decision.

GK VanPatter: It might be that you and I differ on our perspectives towards methodology redesign urgency, but we seem to generally STILL agree on the existence of a methods gap within the design/Design Thinking community and need for methods redesign work to be underway in multiple streams within the community.

Yes, here some of our methods redesign differences are emerging and that's OK. I think what is happening here is that even between the two of us, significant differences remain even after we acknowledge the existing methods gap and need for change. A lot of that might have to do with the neighborhoods we hang out in and align ourselves with.

Perhaps our bumpy dialogue here might be useful to some readers grappling with similar cross-community alignment issues.

I could whisper to you that folks in our Humantific sensemaking practice would probably point out that "Anticipation" is not an opposite to "Understanding". Our innovation practice contains the perspective that both New Pattern Creation and Existing Pattern Optimization can be accomplished via "Design" or various other changemaking methods. :-) Some methods are more human-centered then others. Some have different starting points. At its redesigned best "Design" is essentially a human-centered, or life-centered, changemaking approach. Hey, maybe we can figure out how to teach a class together sometime, Peter! Get our explanation models synced up. I would be happy to engage further is such conversation outside this book. :-)

Taking a deep breath, I might point out that in your comments here you are making some very forceful statements publicly outside your systems thinking neighborhood regarding "problem solving." Since we are here to talk about methods-related issues, maybe it's a good moment for us to address this.

With a long methods-oriented history that predates the design methods movement, the soft systems movement and the systemic design movement, there is probably not a single person in the CPS (Creative Problem Solving) community of practice today who would agree with such a depiction of "problem solving" as you describe. With our cross-community awareness hats on, let's acknowledge this.

While this disconnect is not our focus in this short duration conversation your heavy-hitting statements regarding problem-solving cannot go by without comment as that would not be fair to our readers.

Backing up for just a second, I might point out that we at Humantific know the CPS community and the design community well. We work in both arenas, as well as others.

As the foundation for our own work in this redesigning methods arena, we not only conducted and published 30+ investigative NextD Journal community-oriented conversations with leaders, we researched and wrote the Innovation Methods Mapping book which looked at 80+ years of methods design across multiple communities of knowledge and practice.

PATTERN OPTIMIZING

IMPROVE THE GAME

PRESENT FOCUS

SOLVING

BUILDING

PROGRAMMED

SHORT TERM

EVOLUTIONARY

PATTERN CREATING

CHANGE THE GAME

FUTURE FOCUS

ANTICIPATING

EMERGING

UNPROGRAMMED

LONG TERM

REVOLUTIONARY

OPTIMIZE CREATE

OPTIMIZE	CREATE
EXISTING SYSTEMS	**NEW** SYSTEMS
EXISTING TECHNOLOGIES	**NEW** TECHNOLOGIES
EXISTING BUSINESSES	**NEW** BUSINESSES
EXISTING SERVICES	**NEW** SERVICES
EXISTING EXPERIENCES	**NEW** EXPERIENCES
EXISTING PRODUCTS	**NEW** PRODUCTS
EXISTING PROCESSES	**NEW** PROCESSES

Innovation Ambidexterity Strategic Model, Source: Humantific Complexity Navigation Workbook

THINKING MADE VISIBLE RESEARCH

In addition, during that period we conducted classroom-level research around methods being taught in designerly academies. Published as Design Thinking Made Visible, we also learned a lot about what is and is not going on in academia around design methods in particular. There were numerous rather startling findings that came out of that visualized research, particularly around assumed starting points that have been publicly available to everyone including the design schools for numerous years.

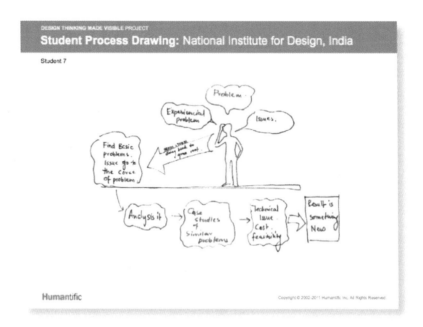

Screen from Design Thinking Made Visible 2002-2011, Source: Humantific

One of the ongoing project streams in our practice that we have worked on for 10 years is our collaboration with Measure of America at the Social Science Research Council, a societal sensemaking project focused in the United States. Its purpose is to make sense of complex societal issues in ways that are useful to policy makers. On an ongoing basis Measure of America publishes societal sensemaking focused at the national and state level. It has become a highly influential series of societal sensemaking publications.

All of that as well as 18 or so years in practice helping multidisciplinary teams tackle fuzzy, complex multi-stakeholder challenges and teaching organizational leaders Complexity Navigation skills informs our perspective on this subject today.

My perspective on the 1970 "Predicament of Mankind" by Club of Rome that preceded the 1972 Limits to Growth that you refer to is essentially a pitch document. In the Predicament document can be found the seeds of the odd conveniently uninformed depictions of "problem solving" that later appear in Limits to Growth.

The "Predicament of Mankind" document viewable in PDF form online is basically a consulting proposal which sought to secure a 1970-era project in the range of $900K and thus as part of its pitch creates a strawman case argument against its own rather uninformed depiction of what it describes as "problem solving."

There seems to be no awareness in either doc that there was and is an actual CPS practice community, but rather depicts "problem solving" as a dumbed-down abstraction in its strawman differentiating argument. It appears that they were actually trying to differentiate against "scientific method," but for some reason they unfortunately chose the term "problem solving."

My perspective on the 1970 'Predicament of Mankind' by Club of Rome that preceded the 1972 Limits to Growth that you refer to is essentially a pitch document.

"What methods does mankind have for solving global problems, and what will be the results and the costs of employing each of them? These are the questions that we have been investigating in the first phase of The Club of Rome's Project on the Predicament of Mankind. Our concerns thus fall in the upper right-hand corner of the space-time graph."

"It is the predicament of mankind that man can perceive the problematique, yet, despite his considerable knowledge and skills, he does not understand the origins, significance, and interrelationships of its many components and thus is unable to devise effective responses. This failure occurs in large part because we continue to examine single items in the problematique without understanding that the whole is more than the sum of its parts, that change in one element means change in the others."

Limits to Growth, 1972

INACCURATE NOTIONS

Unfortunately, the not-well-informed false depiction of "problem solving" seen in Predicament and Limits includes suggesting that such methods focuses on an individual problem, runs in one cycle, is incapable of incorporating multiples of human inputs to create a systemic picture of how the challenges interconnect, and is therefore "reductionist." All of those notions were inaccurate in the period when Predicament and Limits were published and certainly remain inaccurate today.

Hasan Özbekhan, too, was railing against not CPS, but rather ancient city planning methods that he wanted to redesign as futuring. He did not have a coherent argument against the offerings of the CPS practice community and as far as I can tell, he was not even aware that such a community already existed when he was writing in the 1960s.

What is startlingly odd is that what the Club of Rome described itself striving to create - a picture of the "meta problematique" - already existed methodologically in the CPS community many years before Predicament of Mankind appeared and certainly exists today.

Figure 1 HUMAN PERSPECTIVES

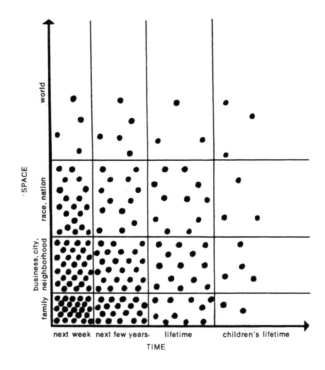

Example Diagram, Source: *Limits to Growth, 1972*

As a knowledge community, CPS has not been focused on single problems defined by one individual since the 1940-50s, as multiple stakeholder awareness and various forms of constellation mapping showing interconnections were already present and published by 1960s. The truth is holistic challenge constellation mapping comes from the CPS community, not the systems thinking community.

The evolution of Challenge Constellations Mapping spans across several knowledge communities approximately from 1939 to the present and is still evolving. Humantific will soon be publishing an overview of the History of Challenge Constellation Logic, and where it came from.

Suffice it to say that nowhere in the Predicament or Limits documents do I see a picture of the "meta problematique." I see very basic visualization of facts that could inform such a picture, but no such picture.

PUBLICATIONS TIMELINE

To help readers place Predicament of Mankind and Limits to Growth in context, here is an extremely abbreviated publication timeline spanning 60+ years.

1973: Dilemmas in a General Theory of Planning, Horst Rittel & Melvin Webber
1973: The Structure of Ill-Structured Problems, Herbert A. Simon
1972: On the Planning Crisis, Horst Rittel
1972: Towards a Systems Based Methodology for Real World Problems, Peter Checkland
1972: Limits to Growth, Club of Rome, D. L. Meadows, D. H. Meadows, J. Randers, W. W. Behrens
1971: The Metaphorical Way, William J. J. Gordon
1971: The Design of Inquiring Systems, C. West Churchman
1970: Predicament of Mankind, Club of Rome
1970: Design Methods, John Chris Jones
1970: The Practice of Creativity, George M. Prince
1969: The Sciences of the Artificial, Herbert A. Simon
1968: Towards a General Theory of Planning, Hasan Özbekhan
1968: First Meeting Club of Rome
1967: The Use of Lateral Thinking, Edward DeBono
1967: Creative Behavior Guidebook, Sidney J. Parnes
1967: The Nature of Human Intelligence, J. P. Guilford
1966: Creative Problem Solving Model, Alex F. Osborne and Sidney J. Parnes
1964: Notes on the Synthesis of Form, Christopher Alexander
1962: First Conference on Design Methods, Design Research Society, London
1962: A Source Book for Creative Thinking, Sidney J. Parnes
1962: The Processes of Creative Thinking, Newell, Shaw, & Simon
1961: Synectics, William J. J. Gordon
1957: Charles Franklin Kettering, T. A. Boyd
1957: Operations Research, Russell Ackoff
1955: First Conference on Creative Problem Solving (CPS)
1953: Operational Approach to Creativity, William J. J. Gordon
1953: Applied Imagination, Alex F. Osborne
1952: Wake Up Your Mind, Alex F. Osborne
1950: "Creativity," American Psychologist, J. P. Guilford
1948: Your Creative Power, Alex F. Osborn
1946: Problems of Men, John Dewey
1939: Modern Man in the Making, Otto Neurath, Isotype
1939: Language of Action, S.I. Hayakawa
1933: Science & Sanity, A. Korzybski
1922: Teaching to Think, Julius Borass
1910: How We Think, John Dewey

In terms of content the Limits document is rather like a 1970 globally focused version of present day Measure of America. Most of the visual models in Limits are depicting existing state of the planet information, not methodology.

Most models in Limits are incomprehensible by not only by today's standards but by the earlier human-centered standard set in the societal sensemaking arena by Otto Neurath and Isotype in the 1940s-50s. None of that knowledge is present in either document. Clearly there was no one from either the CPS or the Visual SenseMaking community in those Club of Rome meetings.

Also worthy of note is that both Predicament of Mankind or Limits to Growth focused on preselected, set of well-known large complex societal problems. The Predicament and Limits activity was not about framing in collaboration with others what challenges might exist but instead they jumped off from a well-known assembly of known problems. That hand-off differs significantly from the vast majority of organizational and societal changemaking work in play today.

One of the things that we have learned in our own practice is that the tools that go along with known problems are not the tools needed when the actual problems are unknown - not just unstructured (wicked), but unknown at the outset.

Let's be honest; neither Predicament of Mankind or Limits to Growth contain any real table-top changemaking methodology. Predicaments relies heavily on the philosophical - don't ask me to explain it - I'll tell you later - but it's going to be BIG and complicated - approach to changemaking methodology. Today, versions of that approach are often being sold as "Emergence."

As you might recall, in our Innovation Methods Mapping book looking across 80+ years of methods history, we did include Peter Checkland's 1981 "Soft Systems Methodology." Drawn in engineering style bubbles, its phased logic does not differ significantly from the much earlier created CPS models.

Figure 5 WORLD POPULATION

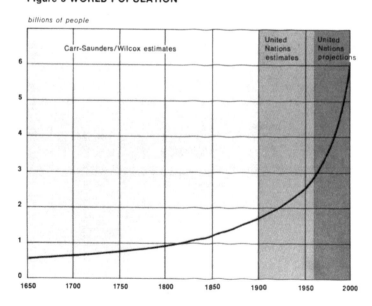

Diagram Example, Source: *Limits to Growth, 1972*

In Checkland's 2009 book, "Systems Thinking, Systems Practice, a 30-Year Retrospective" this diagram below appears which depicts an intention regarding the "soft" version of systems thinking that would not differ from the intention of 1960s CPS., i.e., The process of inquiry in the face of complexity is systematic.

Anyone with cross-community knowledge would recognize parallels between the two communities with the CPS community getting a head start on multi-stakeholder, systematic approaches by several decades. Frankly speaking, it is rather astonishing that Checkland seemed to have had no awareness of the CPS community and its already existing knowledge as late as 1982. Surely we can do better today.

Either the folks who created the Predicament of Mankind document were very methodologically un-informed, or that was a straightforward narrative warfare marketing attempt at differentiating. The methodology part of what they were doing was not in itself sensemaking. It was marketing. That made for a perplexing picture.

The perspectives on "problem solving" put forth in Predicament and Limits are certainly out of sync with the majority of Future Skills Predictions that consistently place Complex Problem Solving at the top of their lists.

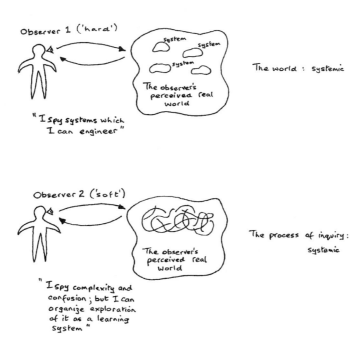

Figure A2   The hard and soft systems stances

What is Systems Thinking?, Source: *Peter Checkland, Soft System Methodology in Action, 1999*

Peter Jones: Hardly anyone remembers or knows about Predicament today. And you're right, it was Özbekhan's pitch deck to the Club of Rome. The reason he didn't win the project that he framed was because he did not have a methodology for addressing the issue of the global problematique. Jay Forrester did, along with the team of Meadows and Randers, and they applied the best anticipation methods of the time: system dynamics modeling with the WORLD model simulations. They won because this was the era of Big Science, Creative problem solving was not considered a serious practice in the academies.

Where I take issue about how Predicament was conceptualized. It was brilliantly conceived as a grand challenge, and the 49 Continuous Critical Problems identified in the problematique co-evolved together as Özbekhan said they would, and are still with us today. What you are remarking about was that hard systems thinkers won the project, and they ran the numbers on the WORLD models to generate scenarios, completely detached from stakeholders or problem owners.

> Perhaps the most important thing we can do in this conversation is to encourage the next generation of students and as well as present-day design leaders to build cross community awareness.

You will notice the Predicament citation also names Alexander Christakis and Erich Jantsch. The methodologists who followed the failure to win the Club of Rome project were the ones to develop the next field of practice, which became social systems design. My mentor Aleco Christakis, along with Özbekhan and John Warfield, recognized the complexity and necessity of ethical engagement of stakeholders to enable discovery of strategies that lead to commitment.

They deeply researched and realized the social psychological challenges in working with system stakeholders, and developed practices to mitigate groupthink, short-term thinking, and dynamics Warfield called "spreadthink" and "underconceptualization." We lose our ability to collectively formulate solutions because arguments arise over the meaning of the problem space, agreement over priorities and outcome, and how actions are implemented. We continue to evolve this methodology, Dialogic Design, almost 50 years after Warfield's application of interpretive structural modeling to social systems problems, exactly of the type we are discussing here.

GK VanPatter: Why this bumpiness matters is because it certainly does appear that the skewed marketing pitch strawman argument served not only to poison the water between these two communities of practice, but has to a significant degree cascaded forward. It has been adopted by the systems-thinking community as its differentiating mantra still today. It is a differentiating strategy that is not based in historical or current methodology factual realities.

The notion that all the ideas for how to systematize "the process of inquiry to tackle complex challenges" are originating and or coming from the systems-thinking community is clearly incorrect and has been incorrect for some time.

We might stop for a moment and point out that in the now by gone pre-network era many knowledge communities including the systems-thinking community and the design community were often talking vertically in silos among themselves. It does not take a rocket designer to figure out that some of that old vertical default bias is often entangled in what a community is still doing today. We are often the heirs of by gone era vertical thinking. All of that serves to block forward motion. Let's you and I get together and begin pointing that out. This is a mission that would align with NextD community objectives.

Perhaps the most important thing we can do in this conversation is to encourage the next generation of students and as well as present day design leaders to build cross-community awareness. Don't get caught up in the marketing baloney of one tribe or another and instead do the work to understand what is real, what adds value in the context in which you are working. Generating and fighting marketing narrative wars is not the same as sensemaking.

Perhaps somewhat oddly, Open Challenge Framing remains the undiscovered country for 90% of the Conventional Design Thinking community still today.

In our minds there is no question that the front-end of the Conventional Design Thinking approach needs to be completely redesigned if it is to become effectively operable (without baked-in assumptions) in the context of Design Scale 3 and Design Scale 4. Simply stated: Design Thinking methods cannot be effectively redesigned to become more adaptive and strategic without a new front-end.

COMPLEX PROBLEM SOLVING

Anyone interested in undertaking that redesign overhaul could certainly benefit significantly from front-end knowledge that exists in the CPS community and has existed there for many years. The truth is most leading design-oriented consultancies have already integrated knowledge from the CPS community, whether they acknowledge it or not. With "complex problem solving" appearing in the vast majority of Future of Work Skills lists, that makes a lot of sense.

Perhaps somewhat oddly, Open Challenge Framing remains the undiscovered country for 90% of the Conventional Design Thinking community still today. It is also nowhere to be seen in either the Predicament of Mankind or the Limits of Growth publications. :-)

From my perspective, there is no denying that the challenges have arrived and a significant gap exists that will prevent the design thinking community to significantly take part. The methodology gap clock is ticking.

Peter Jones: When there is agreement by mass media and mass audiences on a common problem recognition (problem finding), they are probably wrong. With climate change, we are dealing with a system of nonlinear effects from an unknowable multiplicity of factors and causes. When people collectively become urgent, it is already too late to act on urgency.

GK VanPatter: Clearly there is no shortage of work to do when it comes to present day alignments of systemic methodology knowledge communities. :-)

Let's attempt now to turn towards landing this plane by thinking for a few minutes out in front of where most of the global marketplace and design education institutions are right now.

While 90% of the design community, (including the vast majority of the large consultancies and the highest profile graduate design schools) remain focused in Design 1 and 2 scale methods pretending they apply in the context of uncertainty and high complexity, let's ask ourselves a couple of visioning questions. Maybe optimistically get our starship enterprise hats on for a moment.

Is there a possibility that some folks among us should be thinking about the wild possibility that the planet might need a Design scale/context 5?

Considering the many complex known and unknown issues that the global community now faces and a (hopefully) renewed embrace of a sense of urgency (not just on climate), let's think about what the future of Design Thinking/Doing in the context of high complexity might be.

If we can leave behind the notion of magic thinking and embrace the notion of skill to scale, that each context requires a different set of methods, tools, skills, and knowledge, is there a context emerging that perhaps we have not seen before, or is right in front of us?

Is there a possibility that some folks among us should be thinking about the wild possibility that the planet might need a Design scale/context 5?

If we designate communities, regions, bioregions, states, and countries as Design 4 along with all of the complexities that often go with that, is there a different set of skills, tools and know-how needed for addressing complex challenge beyond those considerations?

It would assume a terrain where the challenges are fuzzy, complex, and largely unknown. It would assume a methodological need to think and act beyond the interests of individual bioregions, communities, and countries.

It would involve creating a different approach to methodologies that we presently do not have. Can we, can you, imagine such a need?

Personally, I think there probably is and presently whatever those skills are being entangled in Design 4 when they might actually be different methods and skills.

Peter Jones: The question of Design 5 is a big hairy chimera, and one that we will probably not be able to adequately address here. While I don't like expanding a well-defined model if there's no real call to do so, it must be necessary to do so. But when I teach the versions of the design domains (as I call them) I now include "everything social" into D4.

From a McLuhan media theory perspective, you would create a new medium when the knowledge from the old one cannot be contained in the structures. I have been working with policy and to some extent politics in the last few years. So this is what I see beyond "multi-stakeholder social transformation."

GK VanPatter: Upon reflection of this conversation I can definitely see a need for R&D work to be done on D5 methods, even if such considerations are 10,000 miles beyond where Conventional Design Thinking presently resides methodologically.

I hope this conversation is helpful to readers in both a sensemaking and change - informing way, and thanks again for being such a great conversation partner across the years, Peter.

That's a wrap until next time!

RELATED

Meadows, Donella H. *The Limits to Growth: a Report for The Club of Rome's Project on The Predicament of Mankind.* New York: Universe Books, 1972.
Ozbekhan, H., Jantsch, E., & Christakis, A. N. *The predicament of mankind: A quest for structured responses to growing world-wide complexities and uncertainties.* Proposal to the Club of Rome, 1970.

"Knowledge is a trait of the "complicated" world. Thinking, creativity, and risk taking are complex skills. It is what is done with knowledge that should be prized."

Rick Nason
It's Not Complicated
The Art & Science of Complexity in Business
2017

"If you're a design student, you need to demand a design education that's going to prepare you for the actual problems you're going to face in your career."

Mike Monteiro
Ruined by Design
2019

"If we want to collaborate with people in totally different realms of professional practice, we have to be much clearer and much more transparent about what we mean when we use these terms; design, creativity, and innovation."

Harold Nelson, PhD
Decoding Design Presentation
2019

Closing
WHAT IT ALL MEANS

What is Design Thinking?

Yesterday/Today

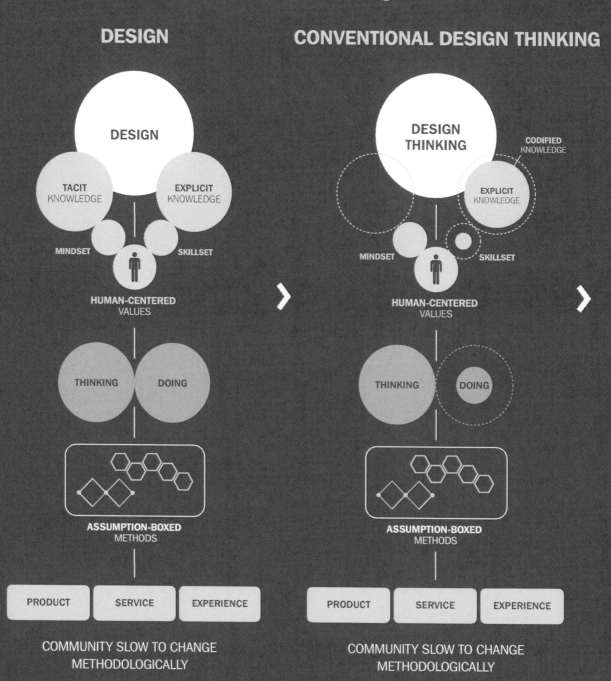

DESIGN

DESIGN

TACIT KNOWLEDGE

EXPLICIT KNOWLEDGE

MINDSET

SKILLSET

HUMAN-CENTERED VALUES

THINKING

DOING

ASSUMPTION-BOXED METHODS

PRODUCT

SERVICE

EXPERIENCE

COMMUNITY SLOW TO CHANGE METHODOLOGICALLY

CONVENTIONAL DESIGN THINKING

DESIGN THINKING

CODIFIED KNOWLEDGE

EXPLICIT KNOWLEDGE

MINDSET

SKILLSET

HUMAN-CENTERED VALUES

THINKING

DOING

ASSUMPTION-BOXED METHODS

PRODUCT

SERVICE

EXPERIENCE

COMMUNITY SLOW TO CHANGE METHODOLOGICALLY

Today/Tomorrow

REDESIGNED DESIGN THINKING/DOING FOR COMPLEX CONTEXTS

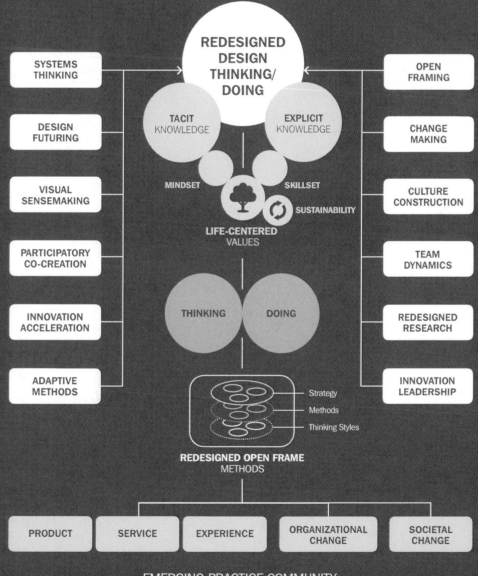

SYSTEMS THINKING

DESIGN FUTURING

VISUAL SENSEMAKING

PARTICIPATORY CO-CREATION

INNOVATION ACCELERATION

ADAPTIVE METHODS

REDESIGNED DESIGN THINKING/ DOING

TACIT KNOWLEDGE

EXPLICIT KNOWLEDGE

MINDSET

SKILLSET

SUSTAINABILITY

LIFE-CENTERED VALUES

THINKING

DOING

OPEN FRAMING

CHANGE MAKING

CULTURE CONSTRUCTION

TEAM DYNAMICS

REDESIGNED RESEARCH

INNOVATION LEADERSHIP

Strategy
Methods
Thinking Styles

REDESIGNED OPEN FRAME
METHODS

PRODUCT

SERVICE

EXPERIENCE

ORGANIZATIONAL CHANGE

SOCIETAL CHANGE

EMERGING PRACTICE COMMUNITY
RAPID/WIDE METHODOLOGY CHANGE IN PROGRESS

Compilation of Community Views

TRADITIONAL ACADEMIC COMMUNITY View	DESIGN	=	Magic Thinking
DESIGN PRACTICE COMMUNITY View	DESIGN	=	Design Thinking Design Doing
NON DESIGN COMMUNITY View	DESIGN THINKING	=	Thinking
90% OF THE DESIGN COMMUNITY View	DESIGN THINKING	=	Product/Service/Experience Creation
NEXTD View	OPEN FRAME DESIGN THINKING/ DOING	=	Assumption-Free Adaptive Methods

Design in complex situations is shifting from...

TACTICAL ❯

DEFINED BRIEFS
AS STARTING ❯
POINTS

TINY ❯
SENSEMAKING

> **STRATEGIC & TACTICAL**

> **FUZZY SITUATIONS AS STARTING POINTS**

> **HUGE SENSEMAKING**

TRENDS MONITORING 〉

USER-CENTERED 〉

VERTICAL CONTENT EXPERTISE 〉

> **NAVIGATING COMPLEXITY**

> **HUMAN-CENTERED LIFE-CENTERED**

> **ADAPTABLE PROCESS EXPERTISE**

INTERTRIBAL COMMUNICATION 〉

CREATING 〉

THINKING & DOING 〉

> # CROSS-DISCIPLINARY COMMUNICATION

> # CREATING & CO-CREATING

> # THINKING DOING & ENABLING

ASSUMPTION
BOXED
FRAMING ❯

COGNITIVE
AWARENESS ❯
LITE

EMERGENCE
CONFUSION ❯

> **OPEN CHALLENGE FRAMING**

> **COGNITIVE INCLUSION DESIGN**

> **EMERGENCE CLARITY**

DELIBERATE EXCLUSION 〉

COOL OBJECT CREATING 〉

DESIGN AS SUBSERVIENCE 〉

> **DELIBERATE INCLUSION**

> **INNOVATIVE CULTURE BUILDING**

> **DESIGN AS LEADERSHIP**

Yesterday/Today

MAGIC ›
THINKING

› SKILL TO SCALE

What Does Cross-Over Look Like?

Imagine that we are going to dispatch a design school-educated design team to go out into the community to work with and help community leaders and community participants with local community challenges.

Would it make sense if the team arrived and told the community that they were there to help, but all community problems had to be converted to the creation of more products, services, and or experiences? Would that make sense?

Of course not, but this is essentially what many design schools are doing. This is what many are teaching. They are telling the students that the tools, methods, and skills from Challenge Arena 2 are directly applicable to highly complex societal challenges of Arena 4. The students are being encouraged to cross over with their Arena 2 toolbox and skills to Arena 4. Students often wonder why there is a disconnect.

To be fair to our next-generation students, look out into your own community and ask yourself how many of the challenges that you see there could be addressed/evolved by creating more products, services, or experiences?

If the answer is not very many then we need to be asking ourselves why the design schools continue to teach this logic, and why design schools continue to build more of these programs - instead of programs teaching skills applicable to the Challenge Arena 3 and Challenge Arena 4 contexts.

We do not subscribe to Cross-Over as we believe it to be unfair to the students and undercuts the need for the design education community to take responsibility for evolving and advancing methods significantly to better align with challenges found in Arena 3 and Arena 4.

Massive, pressing challenges already exist in these arenas, and we need to be RAPIDLY preparing a next generation to participate and lead change initiatives in those more complex contexts. We believe this shift is among the most important change and adaptability-related challenges facing graduate design education today.

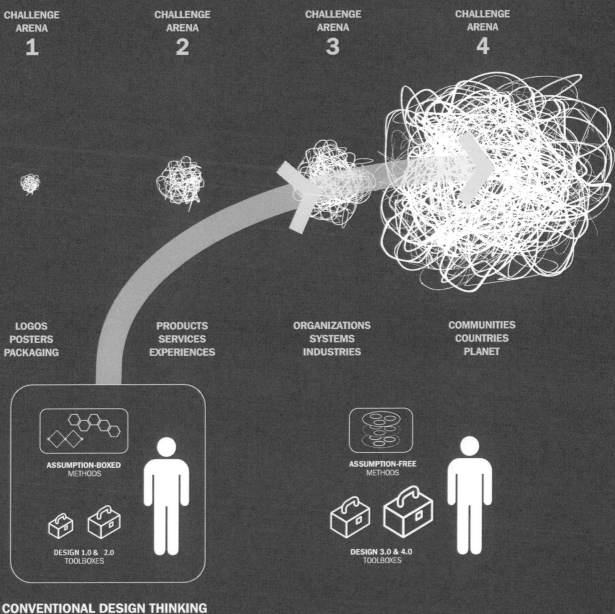

CHALLENGE
ARENA
1

CHALLENGE
ARENA
2

CHALLENGE
ARENA
3

CHALLENGE
ARENA
4

LOGOS
POSTERS
PACKAGING

PRODUCTS
SERVICES
EXPERIENCES

ORGANIZATIONS
SYSTEMS
INDUSTRIES

COMMUNITIES
COUNTRIES
PLANET

ASSUMPTION-BOXED
METHODS

DESIGN 1.0 & 2.0
TOOLBOXES

ASSUMPTION-FREE
METHODS

DESIGN 3.0 & 4.0
TOOLBOXES

CONVENTIONAL DESIGN THINKING
Starts with Product/Service/
Experience Presumptions

In the CROSS-OVER ERA designers are presumptuously exporting the Assumption-Boxed Methods
of Design 1.0 & 2.0 to the much more complex terrain of Design 3.0 & 4.0.

Added Layer of Complexity

KNOWN

In Challenge Arena 4 some of the challenges facing our communities and planet earth have been known for some time: inequality, poverty. homelessness, etc. In this context often Challenge Acceptance, Challenge Embrace is missing and key to forward motion.

UNKNOWN

In Challenge Arena 4 many emerging challenges are unknown at the outset and require robust, assumption-free, open-framing skills in order to make sense of emerging challenge constellations.

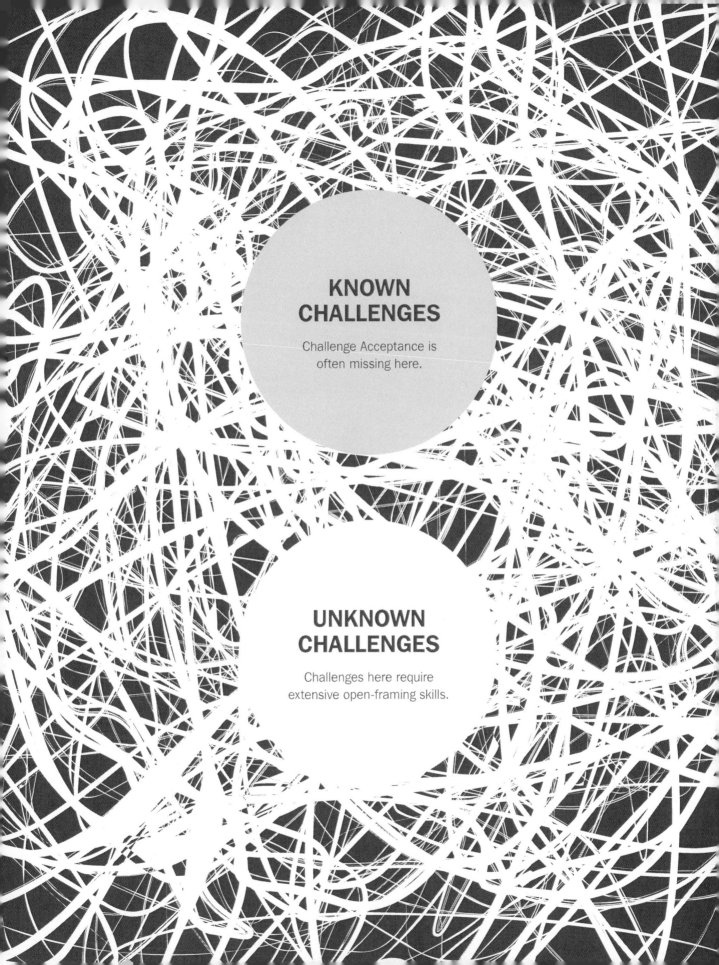

KNOWN CHALLENGES

Challenge Acceptance is often missing here.

UNKNOWN CHALLENGES

Challenges here require extensive open-framing skills.

"Still today, a decade into the shifts described in NextD Geographies, we see **very few graduates** coming out of the graduate/post-graduate design academies with **upstream skills.**"

GK VanPatter

Mapping Method Types

 Open Frame Design Thinking/Doing Methods

 Product Design Thinking Methods

Service Design Thinking Methods

Experience Design Thinking Methods

Google Sprint Method

Lean Start-up Methods

Agile Methods

TODAY:
These methods are
often being repackaged
as Design Thinking

DOWNSTREAM
Assumption-Boxed

25 CHANGE AVENUES
How to Fix Design/Design Thinking for Complex Situations:

1. Step away from the deeply entrenched, academic notion that design is a form of magic thinking applicable in its most intuitive form to all challenge scales. Embrace the basic notion of Skill-to-Scale. Recognize that different skills are needed across the geographies of Design 1, 2, 3, 4.

2. Step away from the now widespread, deeply entrenched, academic notion that design philosophy is design methodology. In the real world philosophy is NOT methodology.

3. Step away from the dependence on packaged "design briefs." No more built-in assumption tracks. In the context of fuzzy, high complexity, get ready for not knowing at the outset what the challenges actually are.

4. Acknowledge the significant methodology gap that presently exists between highly complex "wicked problems" and the current state of Conventional Design Thinking.

5. Move away from the false narrative that product, service, experience design is meta.

6. Conventional Design Thinking Methods require major redesign on the front-end where in complex organizational and societal contexts challenges need to be framed with an open-aperture.

7. Incorporate redesigned approaches to co-created challenge-framing that create systemic views of the challenge constellations.

8. Significantly increase the role of organizational and societal sensemaking in updated methodology.

9. Update/reformulate Design Research so it is capable of informing more than the creation of more products, services and experiences.

10. In the context of cross-disciplinary work process needs to be externalized and visible in order to make effective cocreation possible. (100% intuitive methods are not suitable for this context.)

11. Redesign Design/Design Thinking Methods/Toolbox in order to transcend the limitations of the Cross-Over Era approach.

12. Become an advocate for acronym reduction as that situationally manufactured tribal language mumbo-jumbo diverts precious team brain power and slows down innovation.

13. Step away from fighting competitive political wars with the CPS (Creative Problem Solving) community and the Systems Thinking community and embrace/integrate aspects of their advanced knowledge.

25 CHANGE AVENUES

14. Step away from "Double Diamond" method as it never made any sense in the first place.

15. Stop wasting time arguing that challenges are different from opportunities. At high levels of process mastery there is no meaningful difference.

16. Recognize that notions of reductionism, emergentism, holism, and separability are not actual changemaking methods but rather debatable viewing lenses.

17. Begin differentiating between emergent properties, emergent learnings, emergent outcomes, and emergent (making it up every day from scratch) methods. The three former are not the latter. The universal need for 100% emergent outcomes does not automatically translate to need for 100% emergent methods. In the real world, building deep skills at scale requires some stabilization of evolving adaptive methodologies. Making process up everyday from scratch leads to team exhaustion, a lot of reinvented wheels, and organizational burnout.

18. Recognize that complexity is more than another excuse for folks with no process knowledge to sell "no process" as the "new process".

19. Recognize that guessing and debating upfront if a situation is complicated or complex is not problem finding or problem solving. After the guessing game, the real work begins.

20. Incorporate life-centered values including considerations of sustainability into process redesign.

21. Acknowledge that the role of navigation facilitation changes/increases as challenges scale in complexity and more stakeholders arrive.

22. Recognize that telling a team to be delighted about focusing on efficiency (Agile) is not effective team dynamics or sustainable, inclusive culture-building.

23. Recognize that design of cognitive inclusion, not discipline tags, is the foundation of diverse team making.

24. Think creating new pathways, not redirecting traditional design community.

25. Connect the adaptive nature of redesigned Open Frame Design Thinking/Doing to the future of work.

Today/Tomorrow Future Schools Views

How Might We Create a More Human-Centered/Life-Centered World?
How Might We Up-Skill a New Generation of Open Frame Design Leaders?

Let's be honest. There has been a lot of crap published on this Design Thinking subject in important publications in the last few years. Much of that has been used by other communities, such as the business education community to drive change in their stuck communities while simultaneously serving to stall needed and overdue forward motion in the design education community regarding methods redesign for complex contexts.

Truth be told, the popularity of Design Thinking became an innovation blocker in the design education community. Much of that community remains stuck in Design 2.0 while the world of complex challenges has already moved on. Changing marketing materials did nothing to evolve those methodologies. A decade of slow-motion stalling has resulted in a need for that design education community to accelerate new path creation if it wants to intersect the need for programs that better sync with the challenges already facing a new generation of design leaders in Challenge Arena 3 and Arena 4. It's late at the party and so there is no more time to waste.

Knowing what we know now we asked ourselves what temperaments and capabilities would we design into such new graduate programs and such new schools geared towards Arena 3 and Arena 4. We are happy to share this overview and invite further conversations with those interested in this subject.

The Challenges: **HUGE!**
The Hour: **ALREADY LATE!**
The Stakes: **HIGH!**
The Opportunity: **GIGANTIC**!

SCHOOL OF ENTERPRISE TRANSFORMATION LEADERSHIP
SCHOOL OF SOCIETAL TRANSFORMATION LEADERSHIP

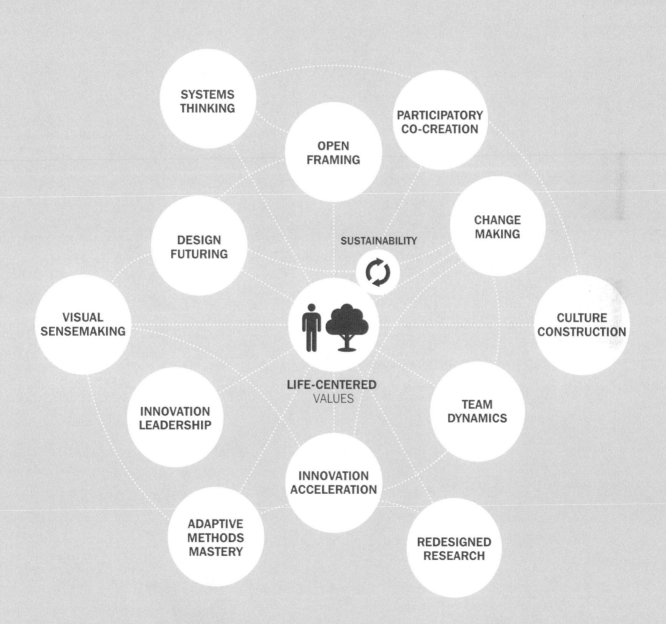

NextD Reality Check Framework

The NextD Geographies framework was created to aid in discussions regarding the complicated, ever-shifting subjects of design and design thinking. The structure illuminates not an automatic evolution of design but rather the evolution of Challenge Arenas that require different skills from traditional designerly methods.

The implications of NextD Geographies is that there is a need to rethink the question of preparedness regarding the application of methods, skills, and tools.

Are you ready to undertake a project in Arena 1, 2, 3, or 4?

Use this simple framework to spark a conversation among your team regarding readiness.

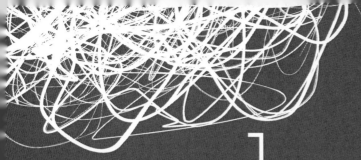

CHALLENGE ARENA 4

COMMUNITIES
COUNTRIES
PLANET
CHALLENGES

CHALLENGE ARENA 3

ORGANIZATIONS
SYSTEMS
INDUSTRIES
CHALLENGES

CHALLENGE ARENA 2

PRODUCTS
SERVICES
EXPERIENCES
CHALLENGES

CHALLENGE ARENA 1

LOGOS
POSTERS
PACKAGING
CHALLENGES

REALITY CHECK

Do we have the right methods, tools, and skills to undertake work in this arena?

Assumption-free?
Assumption-boxed?
Upstream?
Downstream?

REALITY CHECK

What level of skill do we really have?

Skills Progression Ladder

REALITY CHECK

Do we need to rethink, redesign our methods and approaches?

Process Mismatch?

LEADERSHIP PRINCIPLES
Open-Frame Design Thinking/Doing

- Design Thinking methods, tools, and skills change according to challenge scale.

- Upstream methods and tools are different from downstream methods and tools.

- Clarify, externalize, visualize process.

- Cocreation rises as challenges scale in complexity.

- Think constructing assumption-free challenge constellations, not jumping from briefs.

- Proportion of sensemaking rises as challenge complexity increases.

- Data is just one of many possible sources of insight.

- Co-Creation facilitation is a process role not a content role.

- Design of Cognitive Inclusion maximizes diverse team brainpower.

- Process mastery enables continuous adaptability.

- Process knowledge out lasts content knowledge.

- Be navigationally useful in every problematic context.

"Perhaps the most important thing we can do in this conversation is to encourage the next generation of students as well as present day design leaders to build cross-community awareness."

GK VanPatter
Methodology House on Fire?
2019

Who will lead design in the 21st century?

GET READY!

About Humantific

Headquartered in New York, Humantific is a leading sensemaking fueled changemaking consultancy. We help people make sense of complexity and cocreate positive change. We help organizations build adaptive innovation capacity.

For more than a decade+ we have been working with organizational leaders in many industries facing the need for change in the context of an increasingly complex, continuously changing world. Our hybrid Complexity Navigation approach integrates the best of human-centered design, strategic problem solving, and information visualization.

We enjoy helping organizational leaders make sense of complexity, tackle complicated fuzzy challenges involving multiple constituents, and build inclusive innovation cultures that maximize collective brainpower. Our focus is operationalizing cross-disciplinary innovation, making it understandable, teachable, and real.

In our work with organizations, we review hundreds of innovation initiatives, strategies, models, methods and tools every year. In 2017, we published Innovation Methods Mapping: De-Mystifying 80+ Years of Innovation Process Design. Our ultimate goal is to contribute to making a more human-centered, life-centered world.

About NextDesign Leadership Network*

NextDesign Leadership Network is a community SenseMaking for ChangeMaking initiative founded and launched in New York in 2002 by GK VanPatter and Elizabeth Pastor. Each year, NextD generates and shares new lenses to better understand the emerging futures of design and design thinking in the 21st century.

The aim of the initiative is not to change the traditional design community, but rather to point out new paths forward in the context of a changed, increasingly complex world. Since 2005, the NextD team has presented at many conferences and schools around the world.

Find out more about the ReThinking Design Thinking movement by joining the book related discussion group on LinkedIn. You can follow NextD Journal Peer Review Series at **www.nextd.org**

*The corporate sponsor of NextD Network and NextD Journal is Humantific.

About the Author

GK VanPatter is CoFounder of Humantific and author of Innovation Methods Mapping, De-Mystifying 80+ Years of Innovation Process Design. He is an internationally recognized innovation capacity building advisor. His passion is helping to build next generation innovation leadership skills and inclusive innovation cultures.

GK holds a Masters Degree in design from Pratt Institute in New York and has decades of strategic practitioner experience. He was an early advocate of rethinking design beyond the assumptions of product, service and experience. As Editor of the groundbreaking NextD Journal he has gained an international readership. Prior to cofounding Humantific, GK was VP of Innovation at Scient, a Scient Fellow and CoFounder of Scient's Innovation Acceleration Lab. Geared to organizational leaders, he codesigned Humantifc's Complexity Navigation Program. He has long been actively involved in the Next Generation Emerging Practice Community and the Rethinking Design Thinking Movement. He speaks frequently at conferences around the world.

Contributors

Elizabeth Pastor is CoFounder of Humantific and author of Innovation Methods Mapping, De-Mystifying 80+ Years of Innovation Process Design. She is an internationally recognized expert in the hybrid combination of Visual SenseMaking and Strategic CoCreation. Elizabeth holds a Masters Degree in Communication and New Media Design from Art Center College of Design in California. She teaches in the European Institute of Design graduate design programs, the Graduate Business School at ICADE and the experimental TeamLabs University in Madrid. She is actively involved in the Next Generation Emerging Practice Community and the Rethinking Design Thinking Movement.

Peter Jones PhD is author of Design for Care, Innovating Healthcare Experience, CoFounder of Redesign Network and the RSD symposium (Relating Systems Thinking and Design). He is on the Graduate Faculty of Design at OCAD University, where he teaches in the Strategic Foresight and Innovation program. Peter holds a doctorate from the Union Institute with a focus on interdisciplinary study of design and innovation management. He has decades of practitioner experience in designing complex systems and information products. He is actively involved in the Next Generation Emerging Practice Community and the Rethinking Design Thinking Movement.

SERIES: Making Sense of Innovation

INNOVATION METHODS MAPPING:
DE-MYSTYFYING 80+ YEARS OF INNOVATION PROCESS DESIGN

HUMANTIFIC'S Innovation Methods Mapping: De-mystifying 80+ Years of Innovation Process Design is focused on making sense of innovation process design, a complex chaotic subject. With an avalanche of innovation methods now in circulation within the marketplace, sorting out and making sense of the mess can be daunting, time consuming task.

Spanning an 80+ year time period and numerous communities of practice this book offers a new and reusable analysis framework to do just that. Anyone interested in better understanding the evolutionary history of innovation process design in order to better grasp the future forward opportunities and challenges related to methodology redesign would find this book very useful. It can save you years of methods related R&D work.

"An invaluable resource for learning and research in design"
DR. WOLFGANG JONAS

"A rich and accessible tome of innovation resources"
KATHRYN BEST

"Clear, concise and simple. An essential visual companion"
DR. EMMA JEFFERIES

"A welcome addition to the innovator's bookshelf"
DR. ROBIN WOOD

"Incredibly clear and useful"
RAMON SANGÜESA, Ph.D.

"A masterful piece of work"
DR. SID PARNES & BEA PARNES

"Well documented"
LUIS ARNAL

AVAILABLE ON AMAZON

Made in the USA
Columbia, SC
03 February 2022

55355609R00095